Ancient Peoples and Places

SOUTHERN AFRICA

General Editor

DR. GLYN DANIEL

ABOUT THE AUTHOR

Educated at Rugby School, and Pembroke College, Cambridge, where he studied Archaeology and Anthropology, Brian Fagan was Keeper of Prehistory at the Livingstone Museum in Zambia from July 1959 to March 1965. There he carried out large-scale research into the Iron Age cultures of the Southern Province and the results of this work are shortly to be published in monograph form.

Dr. Fagan, who is the author of a number of scientific papers on the Iron Age, is now directing a research project into Bantu Origins in East and Central Africa under the auspices of the British Institute for History and Archaeology in East Africa.

Ancient Peoples and Places

SOUTHERN AFRICA

DURING THE IRON AGE

Brian M. Fagan

56 PHOTOGRAPHS
39 LINE DRAWINGS
11 MAPS

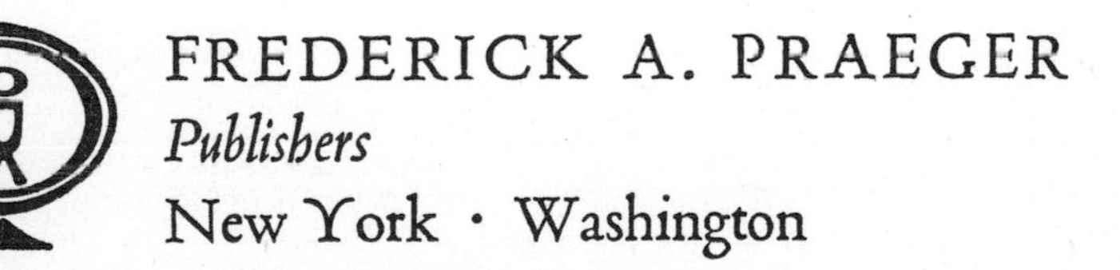

FREDERICK A. PRAEGER
Publishers
New York · Washington

THIS IS VOLUME FORTY-SIX IN THE SERIES
Ancient Peoples and Places
GENERAL EDITOR: DR. GLYN DANIEL

BOOKS THAT MATTER

Published in the United States of America
in 1965 by Frederick A. Praeger, Inc.
Publishers, 111 Fourth Avenue
New York 3, N.Y.

Library of Congress Catalog Card Number: 65-27031
Printed in Great Britain

CONTENTS

ILLUSTRATIONS

PLATES

FIGURES

To Raphael Chewile, Benson Mutema and Gilbert Mwanza

Because their grandfathers took part

Preface

ANY BOOK on African prehistory is incomplete and this one is no exception. Many parts of Southern Africa have not yet been explored by the archaeologist or ethno-historian, and the pattern of research is still very uneven. Many dedicated amateur and professional archaeologists have studied the Iron Age cultures of Southern Africa over the past seventy years, but, for all the work in Rhodesia, South Africa and Zambia, the archaeological and historical evidence for the Iron Age is both fragmentary and tentative.

The Stone Age cultures of Southern Africa are not described in the following pages, but the reader is referred to Professor Desmond Clark's admirable textbook on the Prehistory of Southern Africa for a detailed account of the earlier millennia of African prehistory. The present book deals with the last two thousand years of the prehistoric period, when farmers and metalworkers first settled in Southern Africa.

I have confined myself to a description of the Iron Age peoples of Rhodesia, South Africa and Zambia, and have only occasionally referred to discoveries in other territories, where these affect our story. References in a work of this nature are necessarily limited, but I have attempted to give a brief guide to the literature at the end of the book.

Recent political developments in East and Southern Africa have resulted in changes in several, well-known geographical names. I have referred to the territories formerly known as Northern Rhodesia, Southern Rhodesia and Nyasaland as Zambia, Rhodesia and Malawi respectively. In the interests of geographical clarity, however, I have retained the names Tanganyika (Tanzania) and Lake Nyasa (Malawi).

So many colleagues and friends have helped in the preparation of this book that it is impossible to name them individually. I am grateful to all those who have supplied me with photographs or given permission for their drawings to be reproduced; they are listed on page 178. Miss Phillippa Berlyn has not only criticised the manuscript but also allowed me to draw on her expert knowledge of Shona customs and religion. Miss Marion Goddard of Livingstone assisted with the text figures. The plates owe a great deal to the photographic skill of Mr C. S. Holliday.

Finally, I should like to thank all those who have shown me sites and introduced me to the history of Southern Africa, especially Professor Desmond Clark, who first encouraged me to study the Zambian Iron Age, and my Rhodesian colleagues who have contributed so many chapters to the history recorded in these pages.

My own researches in Zambia were conducted whilst I was Keeper of Prehistory at the Livingstone Museum, Livingstone, and I wish to acknowledge the support of the Trustees and Staff of the Museum.

The text of this book was completed before the introduction of the new terminological code for African prehistory, proposed by the Burg Wartenstein symposium on the African Quaternary in July, 1965.

B.M.F.

CHAPTER I

Introduction

THE LAST TWO THOUSAND years of African pre-colonial history have been of particular significance because it was during this period, known to archaeologists as the Iron Age, that agriculture, ironworking and pastoralism were introduced into Southern Africa and revolutionized the life of its inhabitants.

Since much of the Iron Age is contemporary with the times when the European and Mediterranean civilizations were exploring the rest of the world, there are other sources than archaeology upon which one can draw to amplify the evidence of the spade.

Historical records are a valuable source of information on the prehistoric peoples of Southern Africa, with the earliest written accounts being those of Arab travellers, who visited the East Coast from the middle of the first millennium AD. Ptolemy, in his Geography, written in the second century AD, describes the East Coast as having black inhabitants as far south as northern Mozambique at this time. The Arab geographer Masudi writes of the gold trade, and we know from written records that Bantu-speaking peoples were involved in the Zambezi valley gold trade by the tenth century. Other, later, writings contain similar references. From the beginnings of Portuguese domination of the trade routes to the interior in the sixteenth century, there are scattered references to the political situation on the coast and the interior; these are contained in the reports of the Viceroys. During the seventeenth century, indeed, we have a reasonably complete history of events in the vast empire of Monomotapa, and other historical documents, such as the pathetic reports of the survivors of Portuguese caravels wrecked on the Natal Coast, give valuable information on South

African tribes. In their journeys overland to the Cape or Delagoa Bay, they met both hostile and friendly Iron Age people whose habits were recorded in their journals. In the eighteenth and nineteenth centuries, Portuguese and other explorers travelled into the far interior in search of new trading contacts, after game, or on missionary or exploratory surveys. Their first-hand accounts of the interior are of great value.

Another important source of information to the historian is the work of ethnographers. Black Africa is inhabited by many Bantu-speaking tribes who even today are still practising their prehistoric culture almost unmodified by the imprint of Western civilization. Such survivals of Iron Age practices are of considerable value to the archaeologist and historian who is attempting to interpret his data. One can, indeed, make valuable comparisons between the way of life and material culture of Iron Age and existing peoples living at a similar cultural level.

Many Bantu tribes of Southern Africa, particularly those with strongly centralized chieftainships, have rich historical archives passed down from generation to generation by professional story-tellers. The histories tell of the deeds of chiefs, of the creation of their peoples, and of the events of the last few hundred years. Although many parts of these histories are mythical or exaggerated, they are of inestimable use in the study of the closing stages of the Iron Age. Most oral records do not extend further back than two or three hundred years, but in some areas, like Mashonaland, ethnohistorians such as D. P. Abraham have been able to reconstruct outstandingly complete histories for periods of over 500 years by a skilful use of Portuguese records and traditional histories from Shona informants.

Linguistics and social anthropology also have an important role to play in African history. The study of African languages has been in progress for many years, but there are great gaps in our knowledge and the full historical potential of linguistics has still to be realized. Considerable controversy exists over the early history and dispersal of Bantu languages in Central, East, and Southern Africa, but new statistical techniques may help to give a clearer picture of the development of Bantu tongues.

Southern Africa has been lucky in the quality of the social anthropologists who have worked there. The classic studies of Colson, Gluckman, Kuper, Richards, Schapera, Stayt, and many others provide a rich storehouse of information for the archaeologist. There are enormous inherent difficulties in deducing data on social organization from archaeological finds, but the task is sometimes made easier by a knowledge of the social organization of modern Bantu tribes.

Archaeological investigation remains, however, the basic tool of the historian before the advent of written records. In the past, lack of funds and a low density of archaeologists per square mile has meant that the emphasis has been on small-scale excavations to establish the stratigraphy and date of sites, as well as the characteristics of pottery and the small finds. In recent years, however, more money has been found for excavations, and there has been a tendency towards larger scale work. Animal bones, seeds, and other food residues are now analysed to provide a picture of how the economy functions in its environment, and of the effects which the environment and way of life dictated by the ecology have had on the Iron Age communities of Southern Africa. The latest investigations also include the examination of prehistoric settlement patterns and population distribution.

A number of disciplines aid the archaeologist in the interpretation of Iron Age sites. Physicists process radiocarbon samples to date the settlement; zoologists may assist with animal bone identification, whilst the botanist and pollen analyst deal with seeds and other vegetable remains. Experts examine imported porcelain, china, and glass beads, whilst the metallurgist studies the techniques of metalworking and the distribu-tion of metals.

Physical anthropology has an important role to play, for by studying the characteristics of modern African races and com-paring them with skeletons from Iron Age and earlier sites, specialists can show the changes in physical type which have occurred over the last few millennia. Serological studies, still in their infancy, are also yielding valuable information on racial origins in Africa, whilst ethnobotany is yet another aspect of Iron Age archaeology which is assuming particular impor-tance. Crops are being identified not only from archaeological finds of carbonized seeds, but also from grain impressions on vessels, which have been studied in Nigeria. The history of crops in Africa is complex, and has considerable bearing on the movements of Iron Age peoples into Southern Africa.

The Iron Age archaeologist has to be a man of many parts, familiar with the work of many different disciplines which, in addition to the conventional aids to archaeological research, can assist in the reconstruction of a detailed historical story.

THE DEVELOPMENT OF RESEARCH

Interest in the last two thousand years of Southern Africa's prehistoric past is a recent trend. Early explorers and travellers in South Africa and Rhodesia were not slow to observe traces of ancient ironworking activity and of stone buildings. How-ever, it was not until the Zimbabwe Ruins in Mashonaland were visited by Adam Renders in 1868, and the German geolo-gist Carl Mauch in 1870, that the imagination of the outside world was fired by the remains of Southern Africa's past. At the time when Mauch's discoveries were made, the gold reefs and ancient workings of Mashonaland were being discovered, and when gold objects were found in the ruins themselves, gentlemen of lively imagination suggested that the kingdom of Ophir had flourished on the Rhodesian plateau, and talked of King Solomon's Mines in the African veldt. The earliest excavations at Zimbabwe were conducted by Theodore Bent, a well-known antiquary from Europe. He discovered a number of spectacular objects on the 'Acropolis', including the well-known bird figures. Bent assigned a high antiquity to Zimbabwe, and attempted to date the site by astronomical means.

Two years later, following the discovery of gold at a number of ruins, the Ancient Ruins Company was founded with the specific purpose of exploiting the archaeological deposits of the Rhodesian ruins for their gold content. Fortunately, the operations of this scandalous undertaking were hampered by high expenses and the Ndebele rebellion, and the Company went into liquidation. Nevertheless, it had succeeded in doing irreparable damage to the archaeological heritage of Rhodesia. The Ancient Ruins Company was followed by R. N. Hall, who dug at Zimbabwe in 1901 and became the first Curator of the Ruins. Hall considered that Zimbabwe was the work of Sabaean peoples from Southern Arabia, but he did admit that most of the objects he found were of African origin.

In 1905, the British Association for the Advancement of Science organized an investigation of the Rhodesian ruins by the archaeologist Randall MacIver, whose methods were more objective than those of his predecessors. He firmly stated that the ruins belonged to a period near the beginning of the sixteenth century, with the first stone structures dating to perhaps a few centuries earlier. The controversy raised by MacIver's sober report has never completely died down.

Following upon MacIver's work came Miss Caton-Thompson's excavation campaign in Rhodesia in 1929. She was able to make a more thorough investigation of the ruins than her predecessors, and she concentrated on Zimbabwe, where her meticulous excavations showed that there were at least two periods of building, the work of two related peoples. The dates she proposed indicated an origin in the eighth and ninth centuries AD, with the heyday of Zimbabwe in the thirteenth century. As a result of her studies, she was able to state with the full force of her scientific reputation that there was not a single item in the Ruin deposits which was not in accordance with the claim of Bantu origin and medieval date.

The Iron Age sequence of the northern Transvaal was first investigated in 1933, when a prospector named van Graan discovered a grave with gold ornaments on a hill named Mapungubwe in the Middle Limpopo Valley. Excavations were conducted there between 1934 and 1940, both at Mapungubwe itself and on the nearby site known as K2 or Bambandyanalo. Neville Jones, John Schofield, and, later, Captain G. A. Gardner recognized three types of pottery from the sites, and showed that there were close relations between the later stages of the Mapungubwe occupation and Zimbabwe.

John Schofield was the man who was responsible for the first co-ordination of Iron Age research throughout Southern Africa. By studying the ancient and modern pottery of South Africa and Rhodesia, he was able to establish the relationships of many different Iron Age people for the first time. Since Schofield's death in 1956, little work has been done south of the Limpopo; R. J. Mason has recently published a summary of the Iron Age sequence of the Transvaal, and some work has been done on coastal sites in Natal. For all its sparseness of archaeological research, however, South Africa can pride itself on invaluable archives of ethnographic and historical data, which have been recorded by several generations of dedicated scientists.

Since the Second World War there has been considerable expansion of proto-historic research north of the Limpopo, largely as a result of the work of Roger Summers, Keith Robinson and Anthony Whitty. Post-war fieldwork was deliberately divorced from the earlier preoccupation with Zimbabwe. Robinson dug at the Khami Ruins near Bulawayo between 1947 and 1953 and was able to show by the study of the ruins that there was a widespread pre-Ruin culture extending throughout Matabeleland, into Bechuanaland and southwards across the Limpopo as well. Both Robinson and Summers worked on the stone structures at Inyanga, in the eastern districts of Rhodesia, from 1949 to 1951. By the late 1950's, it was becoming obvious that further work was needed at Zimbabwe itself, in order to clarify the stratigraphical relationships of the various pottery types in Mashonaland. There was also the prospect of radiocarbon dates from the excavated levels. Robinson, Summers, and Whitty excavated at Zimbabwe in 1958 and their campaign there has done much to clarify the relationships between the various pottery industries of Rhodesia, and provided a preliminary chronological framework for part of the Rhodesian Iron Age. In recent years, Keith Robinson has worked on the earliest Iron Age occupation of Rhodesia. We know now that the general pattern of the Rhodesian Iron Age is of a population of indigenous subsistence farmers, who were dominated by a series of chieftainships centred on the now ruined stone buildings, whose power was finally overthrown by the Swazi hordes of the nineteenth century.

Until recent years Iron Age research north of the Zambezi lagged far behind that in Rhodesia and the northern Transvaal. Systematic research did not begin until Desmond Clark's arrival in the country during 1938. He concentrated on the Stone Age sequence of what was then Northern Rhodesia, but did carry out some limited Iron Age research. During 1951–2 he investigated a series of pottery-bearing levels in the Kalahari sand country of Eastern Barotseland and obtained some channel-decorated pottery and carbon samples, which were dated to the first century AD. Further discoveries of channelled pottery were made at the Kalambo Falls site on the Tanganyika border between 1953 and 1963.

From 1956 to 1958 R. R. Inskeep carried out a series of valuable investigations on Iron Age sites in the Southern Province of Zambia. This work laid the foundations for the systematic

Iron Age research in the country, which has been carried on by the author and his colleagues since 1959.

Almost no Iron Age research has been carried out in Malawi and Mozambique. De Oliveira has made some studies of iron smelting and of stone ruins in western Mozambique. In the west, our knowledge of the Iron Age cultures of Angola and South West Africa is negligible, but we know something of the proto-history of Bechuanaland from Schofield's invaluable archaeological studies. Our patterns of knowledge are incomplete, and research has hardly begun in some regions; during the next few decades, however, there should be a gradual expansion of fieldwork into the areas which are now untouched, resulting in a more balanced picture of the whole period.

CHAPTER II

The Land and the People

THE LAND

SOUTHERN AFRICA is largely formed from a great plateau, elevated between three and six thousand feet above sea level. On both sides of the sub-continent, the central plateau is bordered by narrow coastal plains, separated from the plateau by precipitous escarpments. The topography, indeed, has been compared by more than one author to an upturned dish, with the rims forming the coastal plains. The central plateau forms an undulating plain, tilted up to the east. Most of the northern parts of the plateau are formed from granites and other ancient basement formations, the later rocks having been stripped off by erosion. Younger formations are to be found in the Kalahari desert and over the vast areas formerly covered by the desert. In the southern parts of the plateau, from the southern Transvaal to the Cape, the plateau is higher and many of the rocks are younger. The South African plateau has as its eastern border a belt of folded mountain ranges rising as high as eleven thousand feet in the Drakensberg mountains. Throughout the plateau, the topography is subdued and consists of undulating country dissected by great river valleys. Drainage is such that the small streams rising on the higher ground tend to pond into lakes in the lower areas, or flow into the greater rivers, which cut their way to the coast through deep gorges and courses of rapids. The largest of these rivers are, of course, the Orange, the Limpopo and the Zambezi.

Fig. 1

Human activity in Southern Africa has been influenced by a number of complicated interacting factors. Undoubtedly the Great Rift Valley, of recent tectonic origin, has exercised a great influence on the pattern of human settlement and migration into Southern Africa. It extends into the north and east of our area, and has resulted in the development of different cultural traditions to the east and west of it throughout pre-historic times.

Climatically, Southern Africa is influenced by the trade winds in the Indian Ocean, which bring summer rain (November to March) to the coastal regions and the plateau. The western parts of the sub-continent are drier, and the annual rainfall in South West Africa and Bechuanaland rarely exceeds ten to twenty inches. Only in the Cape is there winter rainfall, brought about by the northward manifestations of south Atlantic weather systems. Thus, the eastern, extreme southern and north-western parts of Southern Africa are those where water is most abundant and vegetation is thickest.

Fig. 2

Much of Southern Africa is covered by the tropical bush-lands which extend from the southern borders of the Congo Basin to the Limpopo valley. This northern region is covered with open deciduous woodland, dominated by the *Brachystegia/Julbernardia* species of evergreen trees. In areas where the drain-age is unsatisfactory and the soils are too poor to support tree cover, the woodland gives way to grassland pans known as *dambos*; these are seasonally waterlogged and provide good grazing for cattle throughout the year. The soils of the woodland are moderately fertile and bush gardens will support cereal and other crops, by slash-and-burn techniques. Where their tools and farming techniques were not sufficiently advanced to per-mit the clearance of woodland, the farmers tended to live in open areas, using a more selective type of agriculture involving careful use of bush clump plots on woodland patches or ridges, or using ant-hills. In certain favourable circumstances, they cultivated gardens in thicket areas where the woodland was kept down by the undergrowth preventing germination of the tree seedlings.

Plate 2

Water was of paramount importance to early farmers in the tropical bushlands, so villages were normally sited within easy

Fig. 1. Southern Africa: political boundaries and principal cities

reach of perennial water, and in regions where standing water is rare the great river valleys were favoured. The large lakes and swamps, such as Tanganyika, Nyasa, Bangweulu and Mweru which provide valuable proteins from fish, as well as fertile soil for gardens on their shores, were also populous areas. The highest parts of the northern plateau in Angola, Rhodesia and Malawi give way to more open woodland and grass/thorn bush associations, but movement between the Mozambique coast and the plateau is restricted by the mountain escarpments of the eastern districts of Malawi and Rhodesia. The passes through the mountains and the river valleys running from the plateau interior to the coast were key positions during the Iron Age, for the main arteries of the East Coast gold and ivory trade passed up and down them.

The northern plateau is rich in outcrops and reefs of gold, copper, iron, tin and other minerals. Of these, the gold and copper deposits were the most important. Most of the prehistoric gold was quarried from Mashonaland and Matabeleland mines, but there were significant workings in Zambia and in the central Transvaal. Copper came from many mines in Katanga and north-western Zambia, as from Rhodesia and the Limpopo valley. In addition to mineral wealth, the river valleys of Rhodesia and Zambia are the homes of large herds of elephants whose soft ivory was much in demand in Indian markets. These natural resources were exploited by the inhabitants of the northern woodland region in response both to local needs and to those of the East Coast trade.

For all the mineral and agricultural advantages of the woodland regions, there was a major obstacle to Iron Age settlement in the form of tsetse fly belts, which cover large areas of South Central Africa. The bite of the various species of tsetse fly is fatal to cattle, causing them to die of animal trypanosomiasis. Human populations are also susceptible to tryps, which is generally fatal. Tsetse belts can only be traversed at night, and were avoided like the plague by tribes owning cattle There are three major zones of tsetse fly infestation in Zambia today: the Luangwa valley, the eastern boundaries of Barotseland and the Kafue catchment area, and parts of the Northern Province. We have no means of telling whether the tsetse belts have moved

Fig. 2

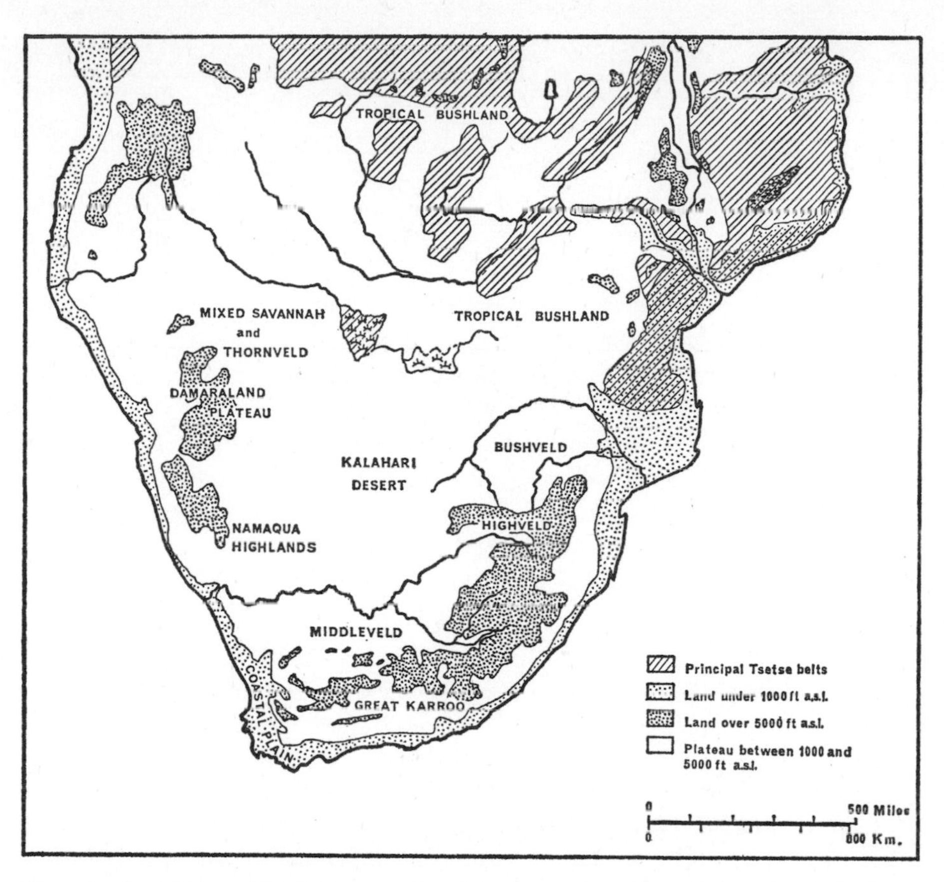

Fig. 2. Southern Africa: physical features, ecological zones and principal tsetse fly belts. Tsetse data from Colonial Survey Maps, 1954

during the past, although there are records of local movements within recent times. Assuming that the belts have not moved unduly far, the movements of cattle-keeping peoples into Southern Africa from the north would tend to be channelled in three directions—from the north down the Nyasa or central Zambian corridor, from the north, also, across Katanga, and from the north-west into Matabeleland and the Upper Zambezi valley. South of the Zambezi, there is a large tsetse pocket in the Gwembe, but most of Rhodesia, like South Africa where fly is confined to the lowveld of northern Zululand, is free from this menace.

The western parts of Southern Africa are almost entirely arid or semi-desert regions. The rainfall is between 5 and 10 inches a year, increasing in the north to 30 inches, where *Mopane* forest is found, merging eventually into the savannah woodland of the northern region.

South Africa is traditionally a pastoral country and for this the physical environment is largely responsible. The country is covered by three ecological zones, all of which are suitable for pastoralism, even if the high summer temperatures restrict breeding and the carrying capacity of the grasslands is low, especially during the winter drought. The open grasslands of the Transvaal Bushveld, Highveld and Middleveld pass into the semi-desert areas of the Karroo. The coastal regions of the eastern seaboard carry grassland and thicket vegetation, which is also suitable for stock, as is the Cape winter rainfall region at the southern tip of the continent. Over much of the country the protein content and phosphorus value of the grazing are low, resulting in high stock losses under prehistoric conditions. Undoubtedly, cattle played an important part in the lives of South African Iron Age communities as well as in the Hottentot economy (p. 31), even to the extent of being used as a form of currency.

In the tropical savannah areas, human and animal disease has been a limiting factor to cultural development above the simple mixed farming level. Indigenous economies today are still dictated and limited by their environments. Thus, as Clark has pointed out, the savannah supports mainly shifting agriculturalists or mixed farmers. Both mixed farmers and semi-nomadic pastoral peoples are, however, to be found. Southern Africa is so rich in natural food resources, such as game and wild produce, that there has never been such a great dependence on agriculture or stock breeding as in other regions, especially as tsetse and other stock diseases combine with generally poor soils and uncertain rainfall to make specialized farming methods impracticable.

PAST CLIMATE

Although major climatic changes took place during the Pleistocene, the minor fluctuations of climate during the last ten thousand years are imperfectly known. We know, from evidence in East Africa and elsewhere, that there was a period of greater rainfall known as the Makalian Wet Phase which lasted from about 5500 until 2500 BC. This is thought to be the equivalent of the so-called Atlantic Period in Europe. After 2000 BC, the climate became progressively drier until about 500 BC, when the rainfall increased during the Nakuran Wet Phase. In Europe, where human activity may have affected the pollen diagrams, it is thought that a drier period at the beginning of the present era was followed by another wetter phase about AD 400. Thereafter, the rainfall decreased rapidly, culminating in a peak of drier and warmer conditions between AD 800 and 1000, but these changes have not yet been identified in Southern Africa. Such minor fluctuations in climate are unlikely to have affected the vegetational pattern of our area very much, but would be reflected, in periods of greater rainfall, by an increase in perennial standing water. The ecological pattern, indeed, has probably remained very much the same for most of the Iron Age and the minor increases in rainfall or desiccation had little effect on human settlement.

THE PEOPLE

Southern Africa is populated by a number of indigenous racial groups today, whose present distribution was established during the last centuries of the Iron Age. Travellers and merchants have come into contact with the coastal and interior peoples of Southern Africa for many centuries, and from their records we can establish the distribution of the native populations at the time of the first European settlement in South Africa.

Fig. 47

By that time most of Southern Africa was occupied by Bantu-speaking peoples. The term 'Bantu' is a linguistic one, and many widely differing groups of people are linked by the common traits of their language. Most Bantu-speaking peoples are dark-skinned, with Negroid racial characteristics, and broad faces with flattened noses and prognathous features. The Bantu peoples are predominantly agriculturalists, and many of them are cattle owners as well. They live in small, settled villages of pole and mud huts and have a complex social organization and complicated land tenure systems. Their diet is based on a staple cereal porridge, which is supplemented by what they call a relish of domestic or game meat, vegetables or bush foods, or insects. Especially in the earlier stages of the Iron Age, they made extensive use of the animal and vegetable resources of their environment to supplement their own produce. The Bantu were skilful iron, gold and copper workers and are thought, as we shall see, to have introduced metalworking and agriculture into Southern Africa.

Plates 5 and 7

When the Cape of Good Hope was first discovered in the late fifteenth century, the southern and south-westernmost parts of Africa were inhabited by Khoisan (the Hottentots and Bushmen) peoples. From then onwards, there are frequent accounts of the native peoples of the Cape Province and their way of life. At the time of the first European settlement, Hottentot peoples were living on the Cape coast and in the present Cape Province as far east as the Kei River and in South West Africa northwards to the Angola border. Modern Hottentots, who are closely similar in appearance to Bushmen, are of medium height. They have a yellowish skin, spiralled hair and a flat face with prominent cheek-bones. The women have steatopygous buttocks. Two types of Hottentot groups were recognized by the early settlers. On the coast the people lived

Plates 4, 6

mainly on fish, shell-fish and, at certain times of the year, on bush foods. More numerous were the pastoral Hottentots of the interior, who lived in small bands, moving continuously with their large herds of long-horned cattle and fat-tailed sheep. They dwelt in small, transportable huts of skins or mats, gathered wild produce, but practised no agriculture. The Hottentots used the bow and arrow and wooden spears for hunting. They did not attempt ironworking, although some of the northern Hottentot groups acquired the knowledge from their Bantu neighbours.

To the north and east of Hottentot territory were found the Bushmen, who were first encountered by the Dutch in 1655, some 230 miles north of Cape Town. Anthropologists consider that the Bushmen are related to the Hottentots on linguistic grounds, but the southern Bushmen are smaller than their pastoral neighbours. Their physical appearance is similar to that of the Hottentots, but they are hunter/gatherers, who keep no cattle. They live in small bands, constantly on the move. As a result, their material culture is of the simplest. Their homes are little more than windbreaks of grass and sticks, and their personal possessions confined to bows, arrows, digging-sticks and various skin and eggshell containers. Bushmen made stone implements until recent times.

From the seventeenth century onwards, there was constant warfare between European settlers and Bushmen. The favourite drinking places of the game were taken over for European stock and the antelope driven away. The Bushmen, who were convinced of their immemorial rights to the waterholes, retaliated by stealing cattle, with the result that there were continual skirmishes between settlers and Bushmen. Having been forced to retreat into mountainous regions, some of the last Bushmen in South Africa perished in the Drakensberg in the 1880's.

The exact relationship between Bushmen and Hottentots has never been exactly defined. They have many linguistic and physical features in common, the chief difference between them being their economy. The origin of the Khoisan physical type is closely related to that of the Later Stone Age cultures of Southern Africa, and the Bushmen are known to be the survivors of Stone Age populations. Many theories have been advanced to explain the difference between the two Khoisan groups. Of these, the most acceptable is that the Hottentots are the result of a mixture of a prehistoric Bushman population with an early migration of pastoral people from East Africa with cattle and sheep. It is thought that this mixture may have taken place in South Africa itself, rather than further north.

Within the areas inhabited by the Bantu, there were pockets of Bushmen hunter/gatherers until very recent times, and Bushmen still live in the Kalahari desert. A number of small groups of people known as the BaTwa, who are thought to be relics of the pre-Bantu population, have survived in remote places north of the Zambezi, for example.

Plates 8–11, 20

In this book, we are concerned with the ironworking peoples of Southern Africa; and for this reason we are dealing almost entirely with the Bantu peoples, rather than their Khoisan neighbours. But in the next chapter we shall outline briefly the Stone Age cultures that preceded the age of the ironworkers.

Chapter III

The Stone Age Background

LONG BEFORE THE ARRIVAL of the first farmers and ironworkers in Southern Africa some two thousand years ago the southern parts of Africa were occupied by bands of hunter/gatherers. Small groups of these hunters were settled in favourable localities by lakes and rivers, or in other regions where the environment could support intensive hunting and collecting activities.

Some ten thousand years ago there were changes in hunting methods which were the result of the introduction of the bow and arrow and other innovations, and the Later Stone Age period began. By the second millennium BC several well developed Later Stone Age cultures were flourishing in Southern Africa, some of which continued until recent times in areas where agriculture was unproductive. In parts of northern and eastern Zambia there are oral traditions of people known as *Akafula*, who were short of stature and very vain. These small people were skilful hunters, and groups of them are thought to have been living as late as 1870. The *Akafula* were probably the last surviving remnants of the pre-Iron Age population, some of whom had begun to practise metalworking under the influence of their agricultural neighbours.

Fig. 3

We know from the studies of the physical anthropologists that the Later Stone Age peoples of Southern Africa were predominantly of Khoisan or Bush type. Many features of their material culture and economy recall those of historical Bushmen. Bushmen living in the Kalahari desert and elsewhere today are the direct descendants of the Later Stone Age population.

Archaeologists have shown that there were a number of different cultures flourishing in Southern Africa during the

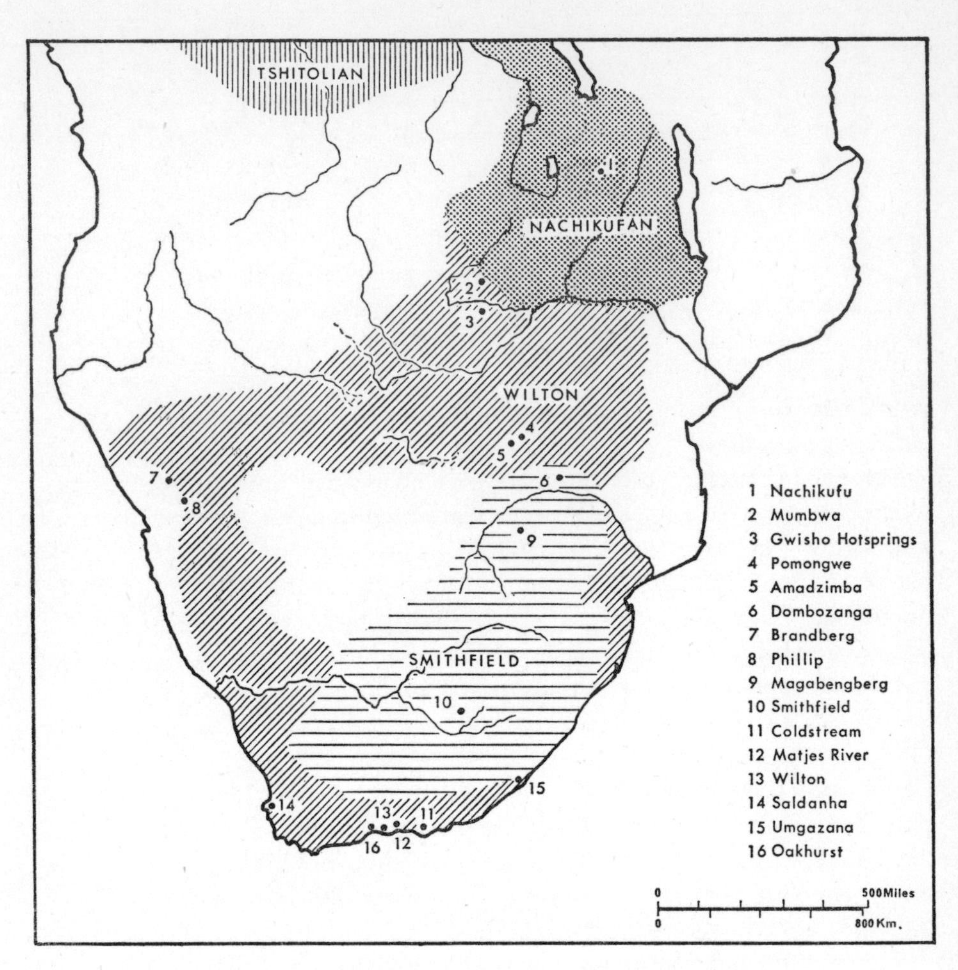

Fig. 3. Distribution of Later Stone Age cultures in Southern Africa. After Clark, 1959

Later Stone Age. These variations in culture arose as a result of differing environmental and ecological conditions, which are mostly reflected in the surviving archaeological record by differences in stone tools.

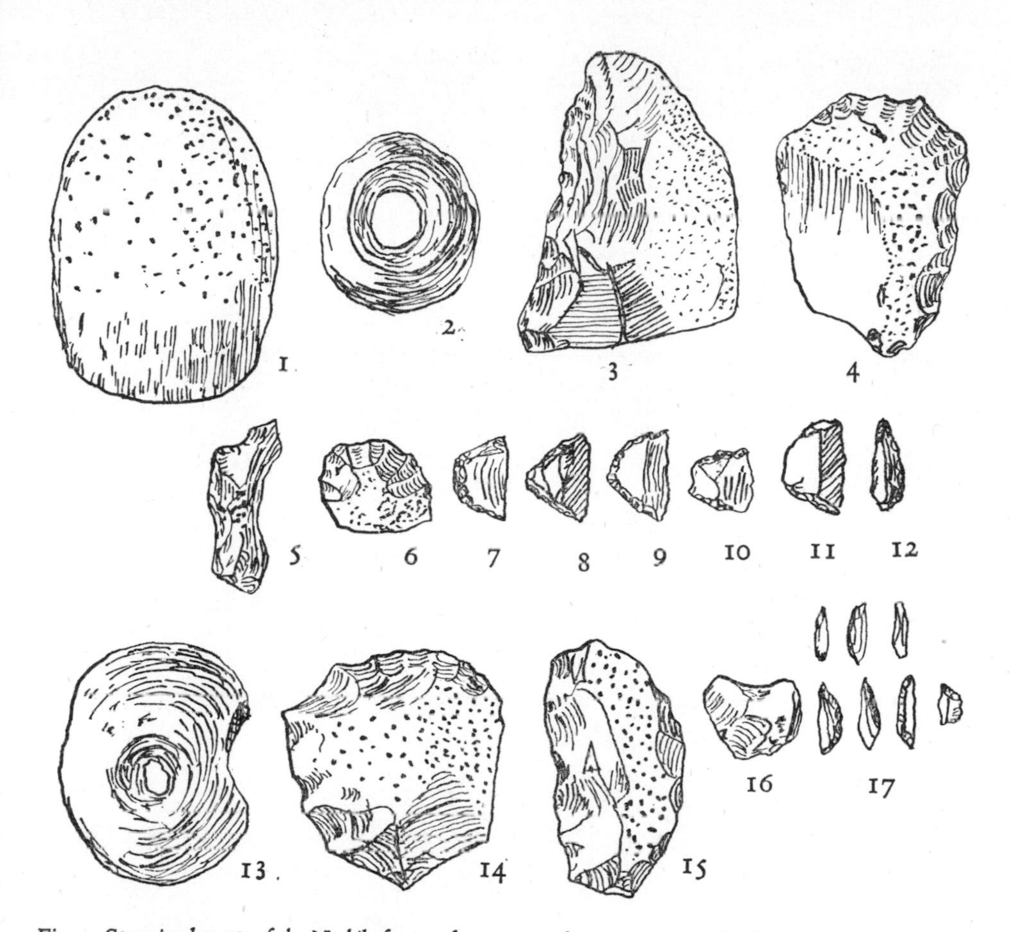

Fig. 4. Stone implements of the Nachikufan people. 1, stone adze or axe; 2, 13, bored stones; 3–6, 14, 15 scraping tools; 7–12, 17, microliths; 16, bipolar core. 1 : 2. After Clark, 1950

THE NACHIKUFAN CULTURE

In the savannah woodland country in the northern parts of Zambia and west into Angola and the Congo, Later Stone Age communities made greater use of the resources of the forest than did their contemporaries in more open country. The woodland hunters represented what is known as the Nachikufan culture, named after an important series of rock-shelters in the north of Zambia. Nachikufan sites occur throughout central and northern Zambia and may be discovered to the east of the Luangwa. Clark excavated the type site at the Nachikufu caves and recorded three stages of the culture. In the earliest, Nachikufan I, small geometric arrow barbs and stone drills are associated with heavier tools used in the preparation of vegetable foods, such as stone digging-stick weights, rubbers and grindstones, as well as pestles for crushing nuts and pigment. At Chifubwa Stream near Solwezi in north-western Zambia, a Nachikufan I level has been dated by radiocarbon analysis to 4357 ± 250 BC. The middle level at Nachikufu, II, contains many large quartz transverse arrowheads, numbers of spokeshaves, as well as polished axes and adzes used for woodworking. Nachikufan III is the top level at this site. The arrow barbs are very small, transverse arrowheads having vanished, and potsherds and lumps of iron slag occur. Nachikufan people were still living in Zambia during the Iron Age.

Fig. 4

THE WILTON PEOPLE

South of the Kafue, the country is more lightly wooded. In the southern parts of Zambia, throughout Rhodesia, and in parts of Bechuanaland and South Africa a different Later Stone Age culture complex flourished.

The Wilton culture, named after a cave in South Africa, has a number of variants over this enormous area. Wilton people had lighter tools than their northern contemporaries, for they appear to have relied more on hunting. Their characteristic stone implements are crescentic arrow barbs or microliths, small, circular scrapers and a number of other scraping tools.

Fig. 5

In Zambia two stages of the Wilton culture have been recognized in the Upper Zambezi valley. They are distinguished by

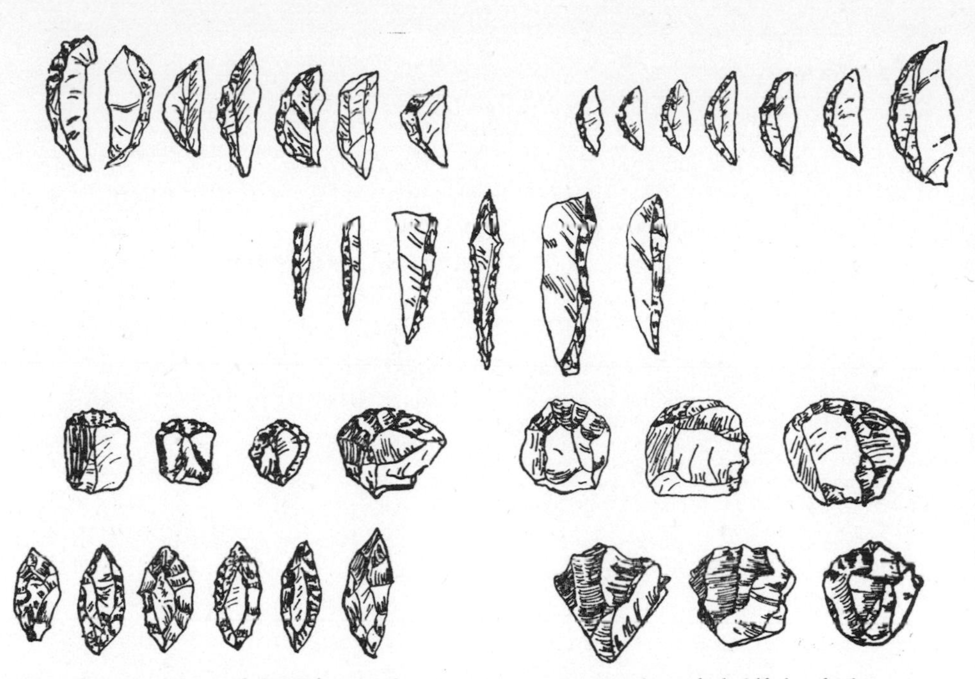

Fig. 5. Stone implements of the Wilton people. Top row, crescents; second row, backed blades; third row, thumbnail scrapers; bottom row left, double crescents; bottom row right, cores. 1 : 2. After Burkitt, 1928

the smaller microliths in the later stages, when fishing played a prominent role. The most important Wilton sites north of the Zambezi are the Gwisho Hotspring sites on Lochinvar Ranch. Three settlements have been excavated and have been found to date to *c.* 2700 BC. The spring water preserved the perishable elements of the culture, which included wooden digging-sticks for grubbing up tubers, as well as bone and wooden arrowheads. The inhabitants' diet included a wide range of fruit and seeds and they were hunting animals as large as the elephant and rhinoceros. Many of the Lochinvar finds are strikingly similar to tools made by modern Bushmen.

South of the Zambezi, there was a large Wilton population in the Matopo Hills, as well as in Mashonaland where heavier tools were made. At Pomongwe cave in the Matopos the early stages of the Wilton date to 5660 ± 110 BC, whereas a later site,

Amadzimba, with fine bone tools preserved, has been dated to 2250 ± 150 BC by radiocarbon analysis. Wilton people were still living in Dombozanga cave near Beitbridge as late as AD 730 ± 100.

In South Africa the classic Wilton area is in the Cape, although the culture is also found in Natal, the Free State and in South West Africa. It has been shown that there were two stages in the Cape, the later of which was associated with Hottentot pottery. A wealth of perishable finds including bedding, pegs and reeds have been found at Melkhoutboom and other sites.

Wilton hunter/gatherers were occupying a number of areas favoured by Iron Age immigrants. Many of the hunters adopted an Iron Age economy after observing the obvious advantages of a farming life, building up their herds by raiding and intermarriage with the newcomers.

THE SMITHFIELD CULTURE

The other South African Later Stone Age culture, the Smithfield, is centred in the Vaal Basin and the Upper Orange, although sites are found far into the northern Cape and Natal. The distribution of sites follows the outcrops of indurated shale, a raw material unsuitable for the manufacture of microliths. The Smithfield is thus predominantly a scraper culture with few small tools. Its distribution suggests that it was an indigenous development determined by the available raw materials and ecological factors. The Smithfield stone technology is characterized by an abundance of various types of scraping tools, digging-stick weights, bone arrowheads, and grooved stones for bead making. Finds at Matjes River shelter and elsewhere show that the Smithfield people made many tools of wood and other perishable materials. A number of Smithfield variants have been identified.

Fig. 6

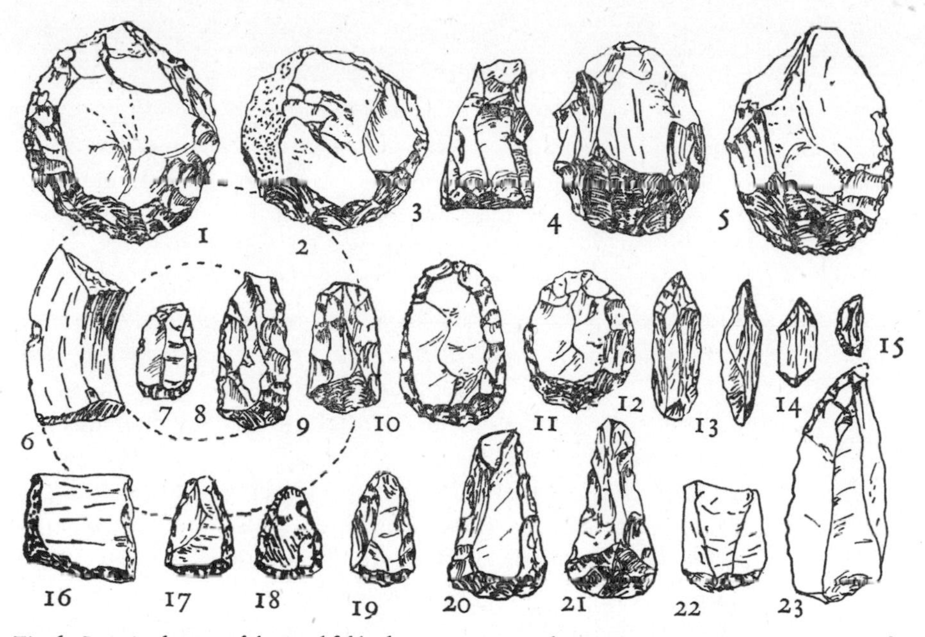

Fig. 6. Stone implements of the Smithfield culture. 1, 2, 11, round scrapers; 3–5, core scrapers; 6, portion of a stone ring; 7–10, 16–22, various scraper forms; 12–14, awls; 15, crescent (rare); 23, knife blade. 3 : 8. After Burkitt, 1928

The life of the hunter/gatherer is geared to water supplies, the movements of game, and the seasons of bush foods. Later Stone Age peoples were thus dependent on their environment which determined to a large extent the size of the hunting band and its material culture. Where game or fish were abundant, groups were larger and sometimes managed to settle for longer periods. Normally the bands congregated round permanent sources of water during the dry season, ranging more widely over the country when water was more plentiful. Some groups lived in caves or rock-shelters, venturing out on long hunting expeditions.

The material culture of the Later Stone Age Bushmen was simple and confined to articles which they could carry around with them. Huts and shelters were built of grass and sticks, many of them merely windbreaks to shelter the families from the wind or rain. Later Stone Age technology was based on stone, wood and bone.

Hunting was the most important pastime of the men, and, to judge from the large numbers of small, crescentic arrow barbs or microliths found on Later Stone Age sites, was mostly practised with the bow and arrow. The bows and arrow-shafts were made of wood, but the arrows were tipped with either a single bone head or a head and link shaft. Alternatively, small stone flakes might be fitted as barbs to the arrowhead with mastic. Poison, made from plants, snake venom, or insects made these fragile weapons highly effective. At times the hunters resorted to game drives and other communal hunting methods. Pit traps, snares, and disguises were also in common use. Animals of every size from the elephant down to small rodents were hunted and meat was also obtained by robbing predator kills.

The women gathered many wild seeds, fruits and vegetables, which were broken up or ground for the pot. In their grubbing for roots, rodents and small insects, the women used a wooden digging-stick, sometimes weighted with a bored stone, of a type used both in Later Stone Age and Iron Age times.

Cooking methods were rudimentary, with much of the meat eaten raw or roasted. Suitable natural containers which could be placed over a fire were unknown. In coastal areas and near lakes, the Bushmen lived almost entirely on shell-fish and fish mostly eaten raw. Later Stone Age people wore few clothes; skins were used as cloaks in mountain regions, elsewhere headdresses and loin-cloths were sometimes worn. Red ochre and pigment were used to paint the body and in many areas ostrich eggshell beads served as further adornments.

Many of the Later Stone Age people were skilled artists, whose art is to be found on the walls of caves and rock-shelters.

Fine naturalistic paintings of the chase, domestic life, and warfare are common and even insects are sometimes depicted. Painting coincides in distribution with the Smithfield and Wilton cultures and engravings are found in South Africa where the rock is suitable. North of the Zambezi naturalistic art gives way to geometric designs. There are several main areas of naturalistic art, such as those in Matabeleland and Mashonaland in Rhodesia and the Drakensberg and the southern Cape in South Africa. All of them have their own long and complicated histories and the paintings are impossible to date accurately, although it is probable that most of the art stems from the last two thousand years.

Plate 3

The environment in which the Later Stone Age cultures flourished was exceptionally favourable. The hunter/gatherers lived a peaceful life in the times before farmers settled on the rolling veldt, but as the immigrants took over the best grazing for their herds, so the hunters were obliged to retreat to less favourable areas.

CHAPTER IV

The First Farmers

ABOUT NINE THOUSAND YEARS ago, the climate over the Sahara desert and in sub-Saharan Africa became wetter, culminating in a period of increased rainfall known as the Makalian Wet Phase, which lasted from about 5500 to 2500 BC. During the Makalian, there were major changes in the vegetation belts throughout Africa, and the Sahara, a desert today, was covered with Mediterranean flora. Hippopotami and fish abounded in the numerous pans and lakes which studded the region, providing a paradise for both hunters and pastoralists. The richness of the Saharan environment led to a free interchange of ideas between the Mediterranean peoples of North Africa and the populations to the south. Furthermore, there were movements of people both southwards from the Mediterranean coast and northwards from West and Central Africa into the Saharan regions. The abundance of surface water, perennial rivers and lakes at the time led to intensive exploitation of waterside habitats. Plentiful food supplies provided by fish, shell-fish, and other aquatic creatures enabled man to settle more permanently in areas where previously he had only been a seasonal visitor. Peoples living in the southern Sahara, the Nile valley, and the Central African regions were not slow to take advantage of the opportunity to improve their economies, and there was rapid diffusion of bone harpoons, gouges and the characteristic tool-kit of waterside peoples throughout much of East and Central Africa. A typical example of an early site of the time is that near Khartoum in the Sudan, where specialized hunter/fishers were living in large settlements by the Nile: their tools included microliths, bone harpoons, net weights, and grindstones. In addition, they made pottery with a characteristic wavy-line motif of

Fig. 7

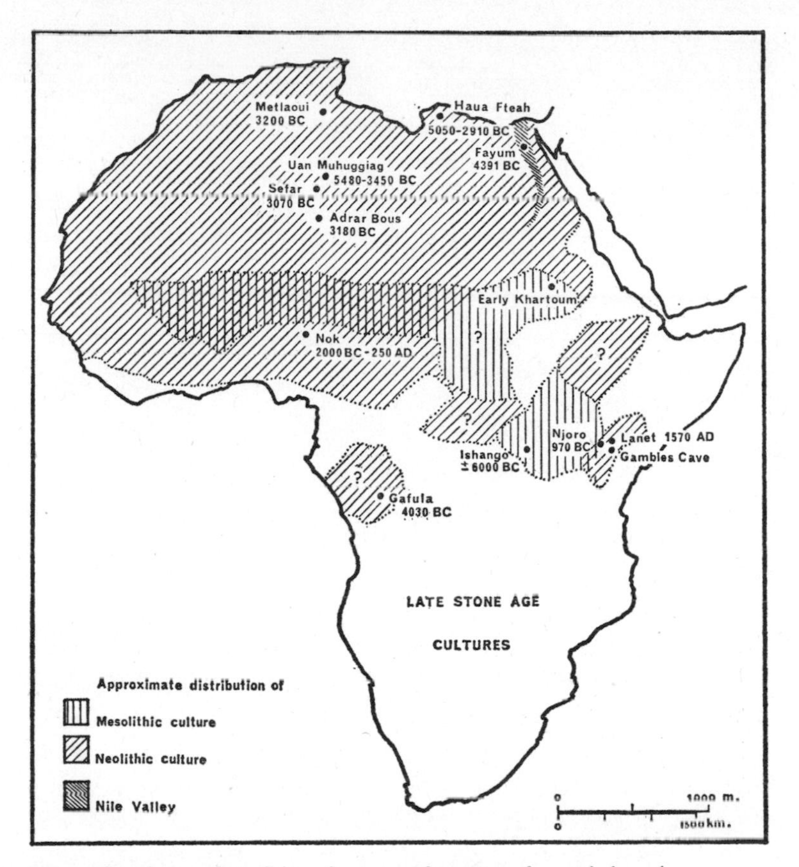

Fig. 7. Distribution of Neolithic cultures in Africa. Data from Clark, 1964

decoration. We know, from the skeletons found at Asselar and Early Khartoum itself, that these folk were of Negroid physical type.

The techniques of cereal cultivation and of stock raising spread into Africa from south-west Asia at some time during the late sixth or early fifth millennium BC. This is considerably later than the beginnings of food production in the Near East, and it seems almost certain that immigrants from there introduced the revolutionary inventions into the Nile valley. Stone Age farmers were living in the Fayyum depression in Egypt during the fifth millennium BC, and several settlements of Saharan pastoralists have been dated to between 3800 and 3000 BC. The environment of the Sahara was so favourable at this time that the new discoveries spread swiftly along the waterside hunting communities. Food production did not, however, spread south of the Sahara until much later. This lag in time can only be accounted for by a number of geographical and economic factors.

As Clark has pointed out, the environment of tropical Africa is so rich in game and vegetable resources that food-gathering communities there were able to maintain themselves comfortably without recourse to agriculture or stock breeding, which would have involved a great deal of extra labour.

When the Makalian Wet Phase came to an end about 2500 BC, the rainfall throughout Africa decreased and the Sahara began to dry up, resulting in a shortage of good grazing grounds. Many of the Stone Age food-producing, or Neolithic, communities began to move southwards to the southern frontiers of the desert. In the Sahara itself they had been growing barley and wheat, which are winter rainfall crops and unsuitable for tropical agriculture. As a result, the Neolithic farmers experimented with indigenous food crops, developing domestic strains of rice, millet and sorghum, as well as yams and other forest vegetables.

In West Africa, Later Stone Age peoples had been practising an intensive form of collecting and perhaps incipient cultivation of wild vegetables on the edges of the Congo forest areas. These more sedentary communities were especially responsive to the agricultural practices of the Saharan peoples, and the Nok culture of Nigeria flourished from 2000 BC until as late as AD 200, by which time the otherwise Neolithic farmers were making use of iron for essential agricultural implements.

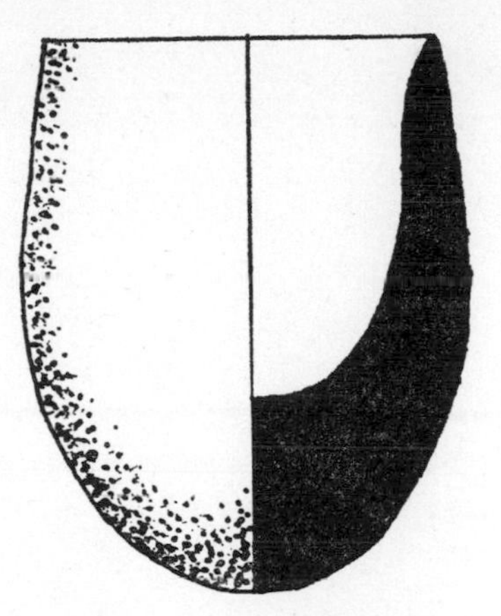

Fig. 8. Stone bowl from Okahandja district, South West Africa. Diameter at lip 12 in. After MacCalman, 1961

Neolithic peoples are also known to have flourished in the Congo Basin, but at a later date than in West Africa.

In the east, Neolithic pastoral peoples moved southwards and eastwards from the Sahara into Ethiopia and on to the high grasslands of the Kenya Rift and Northern Tanganyika about 2000 BC. At least three variants of Neolithic culture are known from East Africa. Our knowledge of these people is gained very largely from Mrs Leakey's excavations at Hyrax Hill near Nakuru, in 1937–8. She distinguished three stages of the Kenya Neolithic. The first, the Hyrax Hill variant, is the earliest occupation on the Hill. Its makers had domestic cattle and sheep, but there is no conclusive evidence of agriculture although we can suspect it from the occurrence of grindstones. The most typical implement was the stone bowl or platter, made by pecking the surface of the stone. Sometimes these bear traces of carbonaceous elements adhering to the inside, suggesting their use as domestic utensils. Beads and polished axe forms point to a Sudanic origin for certain of the Hyrax Hill culture traits.

Fig. 8

The two other variants of the East African stone bowl cultures are derived from the Hyrax Hill variant, the principal differences being in the presence of basket decoration on the pottery. Stone bowls are characteristic of these stages of the East African Neolithic as well.

A radiocarbon date of about AD 1584 from Lanet in Kenya shows that the Neolithic stone bowl cultures of East Africa survived until comparatively recent times, and that Stone Age farmers lived alongside Iron Age communities for many centuries. The archaeological evidence suggests that only limited parts of Sub-Saharan Africa were occupied by food-producing peoples three thousand years ago, and that Southern Africa was still the home of hunter/gatherers.

The exact date at which the first communities of farmers and pastoralists moved southwards into Zambia is unknown, but it cannot have been much earlier than two thousand years ago.

Clark has recently studied a series of stone mortars and vessels from north-eastern Zambia, which he considers may have some connection with the stone bowls of East Africa. These mortars are thought to be associated with the Inamwanga, one of the few Bantu-speaking tribes to own cattle in the northern parts of the country. The Inamwanga are likely to have been early immigrants into Zambia from the north or north-east. In recent times they have been dominated by Bisa chiefs, and the mortars are thought to belong to the time before the Bisa came. Since such vessels are unknown in the Later Stone Age sites of the area or in early Iron Age villages, it seems probable that they may be associated with some early population movement of cattle owners southwards from East Africa. Stone vessels have been found neither in the rest of Zambia nor in Rhodesia nor the Republic of South Africa, although they occur in South West Africa. This distribution has led Clark to suggest that small groups of stone bowl makers moved southwards from northern Tanganyika, past the north end of Lake Nyasa and the southern extremity of Lake Tanganyika, and thence southwards through the Kalahari sand country and along the Zambezi-Congo watershed to south-western

Angola. The archaeology of the route, which all lies over 4500 feet, is unknown.

Europoid racial features are to be found amongst the Herero, Ndimba, Kuvale, and other peoples of South West Africa and south-western Angola. These features may well have originated in such a southward movement of a few East African Neolithic pastoralists who were stone bowl makers with Afro-Mediterranean racial features, and who probably intermarried with Bushmen, as did their Iron Age successors.

Some Mediterranean skeletal characteristics are to be found in Southern Africa's Later Stone Age populations, and these strongly suggest that there was a southward movement of long headed peoples from East Africa. Whether this movement is to be associated with the introduction of ironworking we do not know, but it would seem to have taken place about the beginning of the Christian era, and to have been responsible for the introduction of pottery and livestock to the Hottentots. The characteristics of recent Hottentot pottery are much closer to those of the Neolithic cultures of East Africa than the channelled pottery of the earliest metalworkers. It should be emphasized, however, that the archaeological evidence for this early migration is extremely unsatisfactory, for it was not until iron tools were available that agricultural and stockbreeding communities first moved into Southern Africa in any large numbers.

Iron tools were first made in the Armenian mountains in the second millennium BC. The secrets of ironworking were jealously guarded by the Aryan rulers of Mitanni and their Hittite successors, who recognized the military possibilities of the revolutionary new tools. Eventually barbarian mercenaries in the Hittite army learnt how to work iron, and the use of iron tools and weapons spread rapidly to other areas, revolutionizing agricultural and industrial practices as well as warfare. Iron is thought to have reached Egypt and the Nile valley in about the seventh century BC, resulting in the rise of the kingdom of

Meroe in the Sudan in the last few centuries BC. Iron tools and technology spread widely across the southern Sahara to the Negroid Neolithic peoples of Lake Chad and West Africa from about 500 BC. Ironworking techniques may also have reached West Africa across the Sahara from the north, and East Africa via the Horn of Africa.

Linguistic evidence suggests that the Negro cultivators of the Sub-Saharan savannah regions proliferated during the last three thousand years BC, but they did not move southwards into the areas south of the equator until the beginning of the present era. When they did, they rapidly absorbed many of the pre-existing non-Negro populations. Since the present-day Bantu tongues are thought to have affinities with the West Sudanic languages, it is possible that the expansion of these Negroes southwards is to be correlated with the initial dispersal of the earliest Bantu-speaking peoples. According to Guthrie, the final stages in the dispersal took place from a nuclear area immediately to the south of the Congo forests. These early movements of Bantu-speaking peoples seem to have coincided more or less with the arrival of iron in Eastern and, later, Southern Africa. Sometime during the first five centuries of the Christian era, Indonesian voyagers from South East Asia colonized Madagascar and reached the East Coast of Africa. They introduced a number of important cultural influences in Africa, including the banana, the Asian yam, xylophones and outrigger canoes. Undoubtedly, the South East Asian food plants were important to the Negro agriculturalists, for they enabled Iron Age farmers to settle in the more densely forested regions of East, Central, and Southern Africa as well as in open savannah country.

The earliest ironworking sites in East Africa are clustered down the highlands on either side of the Great Rift Valley, which provided a tsetse-free route to the tropical savannah regions of Southern Africa. There is reason to believe that

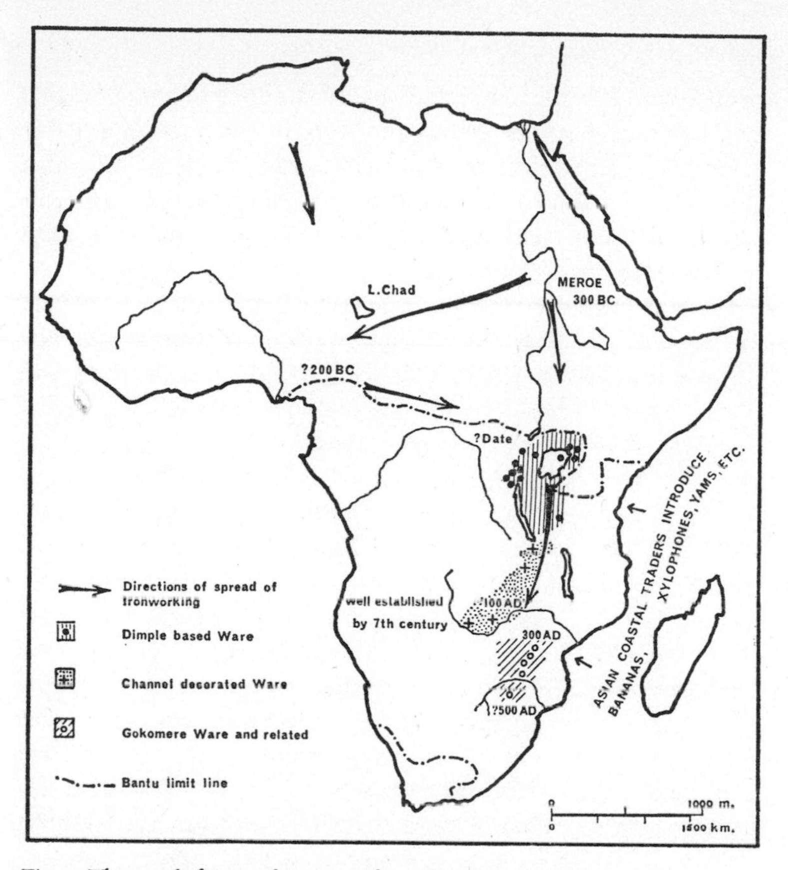

Fig. 9. The spread of ironworking into Africa. Data from Posnansky, 1961

ironworking was introduced into the region as a result of population movements to the south from a dispersal centre of metalworkers in the southern Sudan or Abyssinia. In East Africa, this early population movement is associated with a characteristic pottery tradition, known as Dimple-based ware. Globular pots and a variety of tools are decorated with channelling, bands of hatched incision, and stamping. A characteristic feature of the ware is a dimpled base, made with a thumb im-

Fig. 9

pression. Only one pot of these people has been dated, and that is a late example from Nsongezi shelter in Uganda, assigned to AD 1025 ± 150, but the Dimple-based pottery makers must have been in East Africa at least two thousand years ago, for their Zambian relatives were living in the Upper Zambezi valley by the first century AD.

Fig. 10

In post-Pleistocene times, there were three basic human types in East Africa. The first of these were the Bushmanoids, the second the Caucasoids or Hamitic peoples, and the third, the Negroids. Caucasoid peoples are thought either to have originated in North Africa, or to have crossed into Africa from Arabia. The earliest Caucasoid skeletons come from Elmenteitan (Stone Age) levels at Gamble's Cave and elsewhere, but other burials come from the Neolithic sites at Hyrax Hill and Njoro River. Both round- and long-headed individuals are known. The Caucasoid people may have intermarried with Bush people already living in East Africa, but there is no evidence of Negro peoples in the area until the early Iron Age.

The earliest known Negro skeletons in Africa come from Mesolithic Khartoum and from Asselar. In East Africa, Negroids appear during the Iron Age, but we have no skeletons from Dimple-based ware sites and can say nothing about the skeletal characteristics of the first Iron Age immigrants. The origins of the Negro physical type are unknown, but it is more than likely that Negroes arrived in East and Southern Africa in comparatively recent times and in all probability Bantu languages were also first introduced into East and Southern Africa at an early stage in the Iron Age.

METALWORKERS REACH ZAMBIA

Ironworking and agriculture were brought to Zambia at about the same time, by a population movement southwards from the highlands on both sides of the Rift Valley where the makers

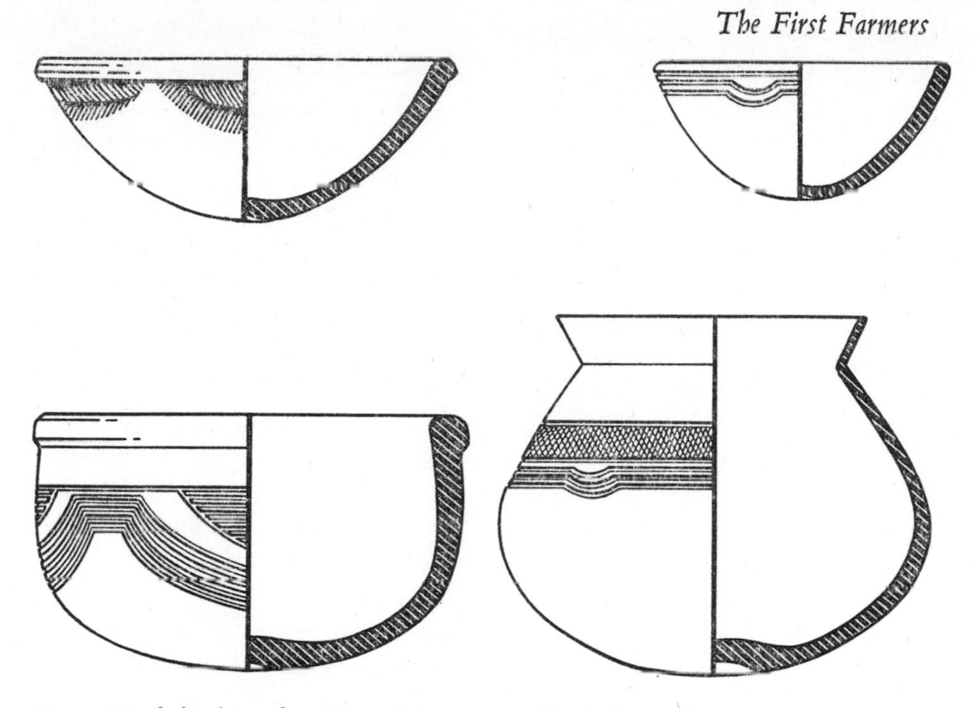

Fig. 10. Dimple-based ware from Urewe, Kenya. c. 1 : 4. After Leakey, 1948

of Dimple-based pottery flourished. Some groups of these people moved slowly southwards, entering Zambia from either the north, or north-west, using the tsetse-free corridors in southern Tanganyika to pass southwards with their cattle.

They brought their characteristic pottery tradition with them, but some of its more elaborate features were forgotten or ignored as the gradual movement continued. Their characteristic vessels are known to archaeologists as channel-decorated pottery. This ware is so distinctive that one can identify one of their settlements from a small collection of potsherds. Only nine sites belonging to these people have been identified in Zambia, as well as a number of Later Stone Age sites which have yielded a few sherds of channelled pottery. The most common channel-decorated vessels are globular pots with thick, rolled-over rims and a band of channelling on the concave neck. Undecorated bowls occur in profusion, ranging in type from saucer-like plates to deep, hemispherical types. There is obviously a close relationship between channel-decorated pottery and the Dimple-based ware of East Africa. In both types of pottery, channelling and cross-hatched incision are combined with bevelled rims and shallow bowls. Two examples of Dimple-based ware have been found in graves at Kalambo Falls. There are differences as well, for the vessel forms in the Zambian sites are simpler, elaborate scrolled decoration is absent, with only a few circular meander motifs present. However, there are enough similarities to show that channel-decorated pottery is related to the East African wares, denoting, perhaps, a common origin.

Most of our information about the channel-decorated pottery makers comes from only two sites. Neither of them is situated in country where the soils are suitable for the preservation of bones. As a result, we know nothing of the racial type of the earliest farmers, nor of their economic practices.

MACHILI

Fig. 16

The earliest Iron Age site yet to be discovered in Zambia is at Machili Forest station on the borders of eastern Barotseland. In the early 1950's Clark investigated a discovery of pottery and charcoal at a depth of 40 inches in Kalahari sand there. He recovered channel-decorated pottery from the same level, and some charcoal with the potsherds was subsequently dated to AD 96 ± 220. The channelled pottery obviously came from a buried land surface, identified by a horizon of charcoal found in a number of soil pits over a wide area of eastern Barotseland, but only one pit has yielded pottery. The dates yielded by a series of radiocarbon samples from the charcoals range from 2000 BC to AD 469, suggesting that the land surface was exposed for some thousands of years.

The archaeological finds at Machili consist of 18 decorated and rim potsherds, of which only one is really diagnostic, a number of undecorated pot fragments, and a piece of bog iron. The most complete vessel is a large fragment of a globular, concave-necked pot with a rolled-over rim and a band of shallow, channelled decoration on the neck. The find is sufficient to show that the site was occupied by a community of the earliest Iron Age immigrants into Zambia. Machili lies in Kalahari sand country; the lump of bog iron can only have been imported to the village and is probably indirect evidence that ironworking was practised by the early farmers.

At Lusu Rapids, in the Upper Zambezi valley, a Wilton Later Stone Age hearth was discovered. A carbonized log from this site was dated to 186 ± 230 BC. Immediately overlying this dated occupation were three potsherds, which have been compared to those found at the Machili site, some 75 miles to the east. Both at Lusu and at Machili, Iron Age pottery has been dated to between 1850 and 2000 years ago, and, since we have indirect evidence for ironworking from the later site, there are good grounds for suggesting that there were Iron Age peoples living on the banks of the Zambezi by the early centuries of the Christian era.

It is hard to explain why there should have been suddenly an accumulation of four feet of Kalahari sand over the Early Iron Age land surface; that it was deposited in a comparatively short time is shown by the presence of later Iron Age sites, dating to the seventh century AD, on the present ground surface some 25 miles north of Machili. The Machili village was built on the edge of a grassy clearing, which provided a good grazing for stock, abundant game, and a plentiful water supply. Iron tools cannot have been common, so the villagers were unable to clear large tracts of woodland for their gardens. As a result, they made use of the dense thicket belts which form the undergrowth in the teak forests of the sand country. Thicket gardens are suitable for the cultivation of yams, cow-peas, millet, and sorghum, especially if parts of the forest were used, together with ant-hills and other carefully selected plots. Such methods of bush-clump cultivation are hardly likely to have led to the deforestation of the sand country, nor are the winds of Barotseland strong enough today to redistribute the sands. It would seem that biological action in the soil may be responsible for the burial of the land surface.

KALAMBO FALLS

Beyond isolated finds of channel-decorated sherds at Lochinvar, Samfya near Lake Bangweulu, and elsewhere, the other important channel-decorated ware site in Zambia is that at the Kalambo Falls on the Tanganyika border. Immediately above the falls themselves, the Kalambo river flows through a Gamblian lake basin, the ancient beds of which are exposed in its banks. Excavations in the lake beds have exposed a Stone Age sequence extending from the Early to the Later Stone Age, most of it stratified in living floors. Overlying the Stone Age horizons is a deposit of red clay, containing channel-decorated pottery, iron slag, hut wall fragments, and grindstones, as well as stone implements. Radiocarbon tests gave a date of AD 550 ± 150 for the lower horizons of the red clay, and one of AD 1580 ± 50, for the closing stages of the occupation; this would indicate that channel-decorated pottery makers were living in the Kalambo basin for as long as a thousand years.

Plate 1

The most important find from Kalambo is the pottery, which changed remarkably little throughout the long Iron Age occupation. As elsewhere, the most characteristic vessels are the shallow, undecorated bowl and the globular pot, normally with a concave neck. Decoration occurs in bands on the neck, on the shoulder, or immediately below the rim, and consists, for the most part, of parallel channelled lines interspaced or confined by bands of hatched incised decoration. The rims of the pots are often bevelled with parallel lines. Stamped motifs

Fig. 11

Fig. 11. Channelled and incised pot from the Kalambo Falls site. Diameter at lip 9 in.

are not uncommon. The undecorated vessels vary considerably in their depth and fineness. In general, vessel walls are thick, and the paste, which is derived from the Gamblian beds, is coarse. In the early horizons, where sherds are less abundant, undecorated vessels appear to be more common. Late in the sequence more elaborate vessel forms and a combination of bevelled rims, channelled lines and criss-cross incision are found. Although the small, globular pots, characteristic of other Zambian sites, form a significant part of the Kalambo pottery tradition, the links with Dimple-based ware are closer, as is only natural with a more northerly site. Two Dimple-based sherds were found in the Kalambo settlement, whereas none have been discovered elsewhere in Zambia.

The layout of the various settlements built in the Kalambo lake basin during the Iron Age could not be established. Lumps of hut wall mud, known to Iron Age archaeologists as 'daga', were scattered throughout the red clays, and the form of their houses must have been very similar to the modern African pole and daga huts.

Iron slag abounded in the deposits, as if iron smelting was an important and regular activity. Very few iron tools were preserved, but they are all of the simple forms found in many Early Iron Age sites. Flat grindstones and rubbers testify to the grinding of grain, and therefore to cultivation of cereal crops. Perhaps the villagers had herds of cattle and small livestock to supplement their supplies of game meat.

Eight graves were discovered on the northern side of the settlement. Their shape was unusual, for they had a deep shaft profile rather than the shallow bowl shape characteristic of other Early Iron Age communities. Unfortunately the bones had perished, but the complete pots and large sherds, together with iron slag, which constituted much of the grave goods, still remained in position.

The Kalambo site provides one of the longest sequences of Iron Age occupation in Southern Africa. It is unfortunate that conditions there were not conducive to the preservation of bones.

THE EARLIEST FARMERS AND THE BANTU

The nine channel-decorated pottery sites known to archaeology are scattered over wide areas of Zambia, suggesting that the first Iron Age immigrants spread widely throughout the country. Isolated potsherds have come from the Copperbelt, from Lochinvar in the Southern Province, as well as from Samfya near Lake Bangweulu.

Fig. 12

Some Later Stone Age sites in the Middle Zambezi valley have yielded channelled potsherds, as if there was sporadic contact and perhaps trading between the newcomers and their Stone Age neighbours.

Almost nothing is known of the economy of the earliest agriculturalists. In Rhodesia, their contemporaries are known to have cultivated cereal crops and to have kept herds of small livestock, if not cattle, and in all probability the channel-decorated pottery makers were doing the same. Millet, sorghum,

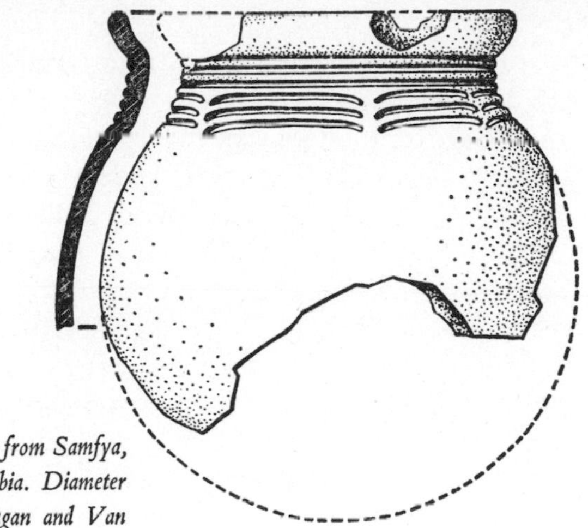

Fig. 12. Channelled pot from Samfya, Lake Bangweulu, Zambia. Diameter at lip $5\frac{1}{4}$ in. After Fagan and Van Noten, 1964

cow-peas and certain species of ground-beans and cucurbits were probably introduced into Southern Africa by the channel-decorated pottery people, and cultivated in small gardens on the edges of woodland, and on ant-hills and other carefully selected plots. The first farmers must still have relied to a great extent on natural vegetable resources and game meat to supplement their basic porridge diet.

Unfortunately no human remains have yet been found in a channel-decorated pottery site, and the racial type of the earliest farmers is unknown. In general terms the material culture and economy of the first Zambian Iron Age people are similar to those of known Bantu-speaking, Negroid communities. There is general agreement among archaeologists that iron-working and agriculture were, in all probability, introduced into Southern Africa by small numbers of Negroid people, whose language may possibly have been some early form of Bantu.

RHODESIA

We know considerably more about the earliest Iron Age peoples of Rhodesia, where more Iron Age sites have been investigated than north of the Zambezi. Mashonaland has yielded most of the evidence for early ironworkers, but important discoveries have also been made in the west.

GOKOMERE AND MABVENI

The Tunnel Cave at Gokomere near Fort Victoria was excavated in the late 1930's, and yielded a layer of Iron Age occupation overlying a Stone Age horizon. Sherds from the Iron Age levels were recognized as being of early date and similar material was found in the lowest layer on the Zimbabwe Acropolis in 1958. The vessels have thick walls, which show clear traces of imperfect firing. Many shouldered pots with concave necks were made, and adorned with raised bands of stamped or incised impressions and lines of channelling. Bowls were also used. These were more often than not undecorated, with a considerable variety of shapes, including both spherical and flattened examples. Spouts were sometimes made at Gokomere itself, but were never in common use.

Fig. 13

This type of pottery has been found widely dispersed over Mashonaland. It also occurs in Matabeleland, where its features are to be found in early Leopard's Kopje pottery industries, to which we shall return later. The Gokomere occupation, which is known at Zimbabwe as Period I, was traced in the lowest levels of the Acropolis excavations. The pottery was found in an ochreous hill-earth resting on the rock of the hill. The Iron Age people were preceded by Middle and Later Stone Age tribesmen. Finds from the earliest period at Zimbabwe are confined to pottery and lumps of daga. No structures or traces of stone wall buildings have been found, and Robinson considers that the Period I occupation of the Acropolis may have been considerably longer than appears from the excavation. The richest middens could well be buried in the central area of the hill under tons of stones and other debris.

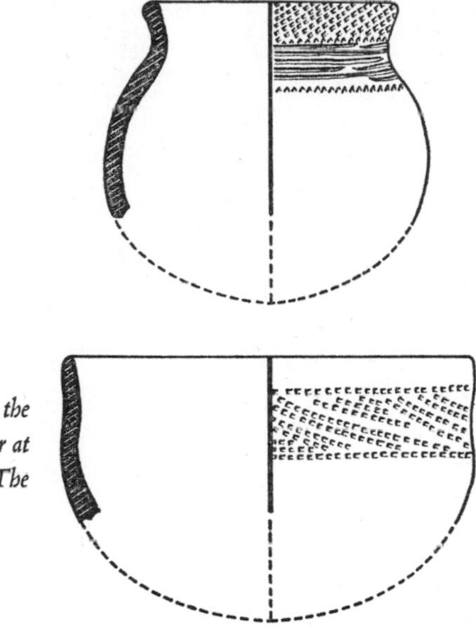

Fig. 13. Gokomere ware from the Tunnel Cave, Gokomere. Diameter at lip of larger pot 9 in. Collection: The Livingstone Museum

A radiocarbon sample for the *end* of Period I at Zimbabwe, has given a date of AD 320 ± 150. At Gokomere, the base of the early Iron Age level has been dated at AD 530 ± 120. A late site at Malapati near the Nuanetsi River has given a reading of AD 840 ± 100.

We still do not know very much about the material culture and economic practices of the Gokomere culture people, but some information has come to light from recent excavations at the Mabveni site, which lies about two miles west of the Government offices at Chibi, south-west of Fort Victoria in Mashonaland. Traces of an old village site can be seen over several acres, and consist of remains of daga structures and isolated middens, one of which, some 12 to 14 inches deep, yielded most of the finds. Two piles of daga were investigated and both of them proved interesting. The first was thought to be a storage granary, built of mud and sticks, resting on a timber framework on four stones. This was, in many respects, similar to a modern structure of this type, indicating the essential conservatism of Iron Age architects. The other structure was thought by Robinson to resemble a hut with a door facing south-west, but his reconstruction is tentative.

Robinson considers it certain that the Mabveni people practised agriculture, although no seeds were found at the site. The extent of their agricultural operations was probably determined by their simple iron tools and the lack of fertile soil. We know that the Mabveni people kept domestic livestock, for two immature sheep mandibles were found in the faunal collections. No cattle remains were identified, but it is probable that the inhabitants of the village possessed them. The Mabveni people hunted buffalo, impala, wildebeest and zebra; food gathering must also have been an important activity to supplement their cereal crops.

Iron fragments were rare, although slag and 'tuyère' were common. Except for some iron beads, no finished pieces were found. Ten copper beads were discovered, and some bangle fragments came from Gokomere, but metalworking cannot have been practised intensively. Bone was occasionally used to make awls or points, which seems to indicate that metal-tipped weapons were rare.

Clay figures of both animals and humans were found at Gokomere and Mabveni, although most of them are too fragmentary for positive identification. At the Tunnel Cave, a mamillated object in clay was found in the same deposit as some human figurines and a clay spoon. Robinson has suggested that these may be traces of the paraphernalia of some form of initiation school, for there are strong indications that Iron Age ritual practices were well-developed by this period.

Fig. 14

The Gokomere people and their pottery tradition spread widely over Rhodesia. Some of the characteristic features of their pottery are found in the earliest Matabeleland Iron Age

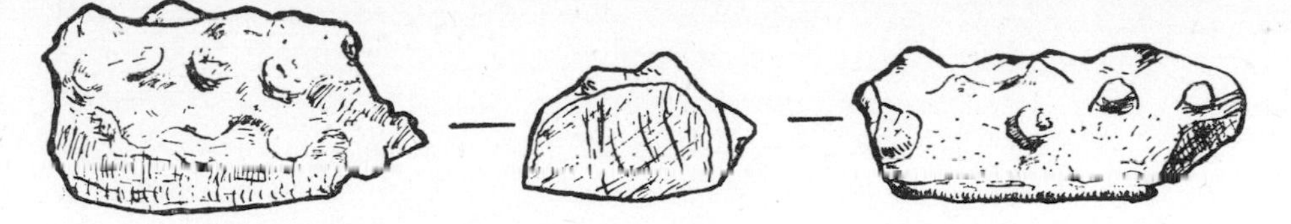

Fig. 14. Mammilated clay object from Tunnel Cave, Gokomere. 1 : 2. After Robinson, 1963

sites. We do not know how far south the Gokomere people spread, but channelled and stamped pottery is known from Bechuanaland and also from the northern Transvaal, South Africa. Many years ago, de Waal collected a series of sherds from a site at Matokoma, 13 miles west of Louis Trichardt, south of the Zoutpansberg Mountains. The Matokoma pottery is related to the late Gokomere pottery from Malapati, radiocarbon dated to the ninth century. It would seem that Iron Age peoples were pressing southwards into the highveld of South Africa in the late first millennium, if not earlier. The central and southern Transvaal is admirable cattle country and would have been suitable for early Iron Age farmers, who relied on their herds rather than their agriculture to stabilize their economy, although elsewhere in the Transvaal there is no evidence of this early pottery tradition. The Iron Age wares found at Tafelkop and in the Uitkomst cave in the southern Transvaal bear no relation to Gokomere pottery, and the sites are later. Although, therefore, we know that Gokomere culture peoples did penetrate south of the Limpopo, we must await further discoveries before we can tell how far southward they managed to settle.

ZIWA

Another form of channelled and stamped pottery is found in the eastern districts of Rhodesia. The makers of this ware obviously practised a very similar economy to that of the Gokomere peoples, with regional differences resulting from environmental factors. Since the first important sites where this pottery was found were discovered on Ziwa farm near Inyanga, this characteristic pottery has been named Ziwa ware.

The distribution of Ziwa settlements is imperfectly known. Many sites are concentrated by the headwaters of the Mazoe and its tributaries, and the pottery has also been discovered in caves and ancient workings. Ziwa ware has been found as far west as Arcturus, and occurs in northern Mashonaland, perhaps as far north as the Zambezi escarpment.

Fig. 16

Undoubtedly there are many features in common between Gokomere and Ziwa pottery. Shouldered pots with channelled and stamped decoration are common to both, but the Ziwa bowl forms tend to be more elaborate, with many different types of rim. In general, the standard of firing of Ziwa vessels is better, and the decoration more lavish than on Gokomere pottery. Although several stages of Ziwa ware have been postulated, many more sites will have to be excavated before the development of these eastern communities is understood in any detail.

Fig. 15

Bernhard has obtained a series of important radiocarbon dates for Ziwa sites. His earliest date, of AD 300 ± 100, comes from a grave on Ziwa farm itself. Three other dates of AD 850 ± 100, 900 ± 100, and 1010 ± 110 respectively show that Ziwa ware was still being made at the beginning of the second millennium. The earliest Ziwa sample is in fact the earliest Iron Age date from Rhodesia at the time of writing. Undoubtedly, however, the Gokomere and Ziwa peoples were broadly contemporary with each other, and, judging from their pottery, were of common origin.

THE EARLIEST RHODESIAN FARMERS

We have shown that most of Rhodesia's earliest farmers were practising a basically similar economy, with a simple material culture and common pottery tradition, but there were regional

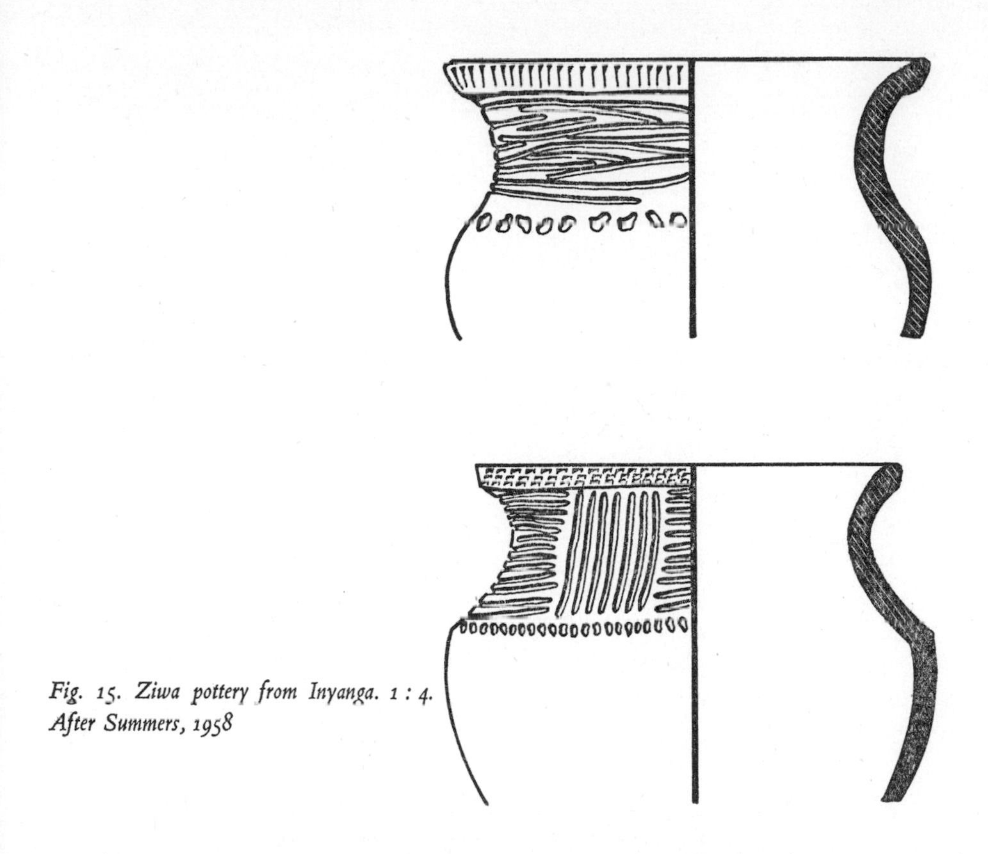

Fig. 15. Ziwa pottery from Inyanga. 1 : 4. After Summers, 1958

variations both in the east and west of the country. There is general agreement that these early Rhodesian farmers made vessels which can be connected with the earliest pottery in the north. Both the use of irregular channelling and of oblique stamping on the rim of pots serve to connect Gokomere ware with Zambian channelled pottery. Bowls are a common feature of both Dimple-based and channel-decorated industries.

We cannot emphasize too strongly the profound influence of the earliest Rhodesian Iron Age people on their descendants. The decorative motifs on their pots, their mining techniques, as well as ritual and economic practices, were inherited, and modified, by their successors. In later centuries, the descendants of the original farming tribes were dominated by a series of powerful chieftainly families, whose power was based on the mining ability and economic skill of the indigenous pastoral and agricultural peoples of Rhodesia who had arrived from the north many centuries before then.

THE IRON AGE REVOLUTION

Gradually, Iron Age communities pushed southwards in small groups, reaching the Zambezi by the early centuries of the Christian era, settling in Mashonaland by the fourth century, and crossing the Limpopo some time later. We know from the skeletons in the Ziwa graves on Ziwa farm that a proportion of the population was Negroid, but these features were diluted by intermarriage with Bush peoples already living in Rhodesia in Later Stone Age times. We know too, from the archaeological record and oral traditions, as well as from modern examples, that Stone Age hunter/gatherers lived in peaceful association with Iron Age farmers until recent times. The powerful influence of the new immigrants on their neighbours must have led many of the latter to abandon their traditional way of life and to turn to food producing. This was not an immediate change, but a gradual process of acculturation, which was still in progress when the Iron Age ended. Many of the economic practices of the Stone Age were adopted by the new immigrants, and much of the botanical knowledge of the present tribes of Southern Africa, for example, must be derived from Stone Age sources.

CHAPTER V

Subsistence Farmers in Zambia:
c. AD 400–1200

IRON AGE COMMUNITIES were scattered throughout Zambia within a few centuries of the arrival of the first farmers on the banks of the Zambezi. As we have seen, many Stone Age hunters were not slow to adopt the economy and material standards of their more fortunate neighbours, resulting in a rapid diffusion of Iron Age culture throughout the territory.

The radiocarbon dates at the Kalambo Falls show that channel-decorated pottery makers, direct descendants of the first farmers, were farming in the northern parts of Zambia in the middle of the second millennium AD, and were only disturbed by the arrival of peoples from the Congo Basin in the last five hundred years of the Iron Age (pp. 54, 146). A rather similar state of affairs may have existed east of the Luangwa, where the earliest recorded population movements are those of the Chewa and Maravi in the sixteenth century.

In the southern and north-western parts of Zambia, the earliest farmers were absorbed or replaced by new Iron Age peoples during the first thousand years of the Iron Age. We can still only guess at the events which took place. The channelled pottery tradition seems to have been replaced by new potting habits, which may be a reflection either of regional variations developing amongst the original farming population, or of the influence of immigrants from other areas.

The Batoka plateau, confined by the Kafue and Zambezi valleys, was probably one of the most favourable areas for Iron Age settlement in Zambia. It is comparatively cool, free of tsetse flies, and well watered. The frequent areas of watershed grassland and many grassy clearings make it particularly suitable for pastoral communities with only a few iron tools. A number of Iron Age cultures have been identified on the plateau within recent years, and these have told us much about the economics of early Iron Age farming.

Fig. 16

DAMBWA

A large Iron Age site was found on the edge of a clearing named Dambwa, three miles north of Livingstone, in 1962. The settlement was investigated by Daniels, who estimated that it dated to about AD 400. Pottery, iron slag, the occasional metal object, and traces of daga structures were found in a culture layer some 30 inches deep. The village must have been a large one, for discoloured soil and pottery occur over an area about 100 yards in diameter.

No complete houses were discovered, but piles of wall rubble and patches of mud floors are scattered in the deposits. There is every indication that the huts at Dambwa were similar to modern African examples. The inhabitants dug storage pits into the sand, which were probably lined to protect the contents from termites.

Iron slag is so abundant at Dambwa that ironworking must have been an extremely important activity. Some small arrowheads with simple blades were found, as were a finger ring and some strips of copper wire and bangles, the only imported objects in the village.

The dead were buried within the settlement, with the contracted bodies squashed into small grave pits. Three burials have been found at Dambwa, and these show a mixture of Negro and Bush features.

Dambwa pottery combines a number of different elements. Many vessels bear the channelled decoration, stamped rims, and other features found on the earliest Iron Age wares of Rhodesia. Shouldered pots are the most common receptacles, but bowls are also found. The Machili pot form has not been found at Dambwa, but there can be no doubt that many

Fig. 17

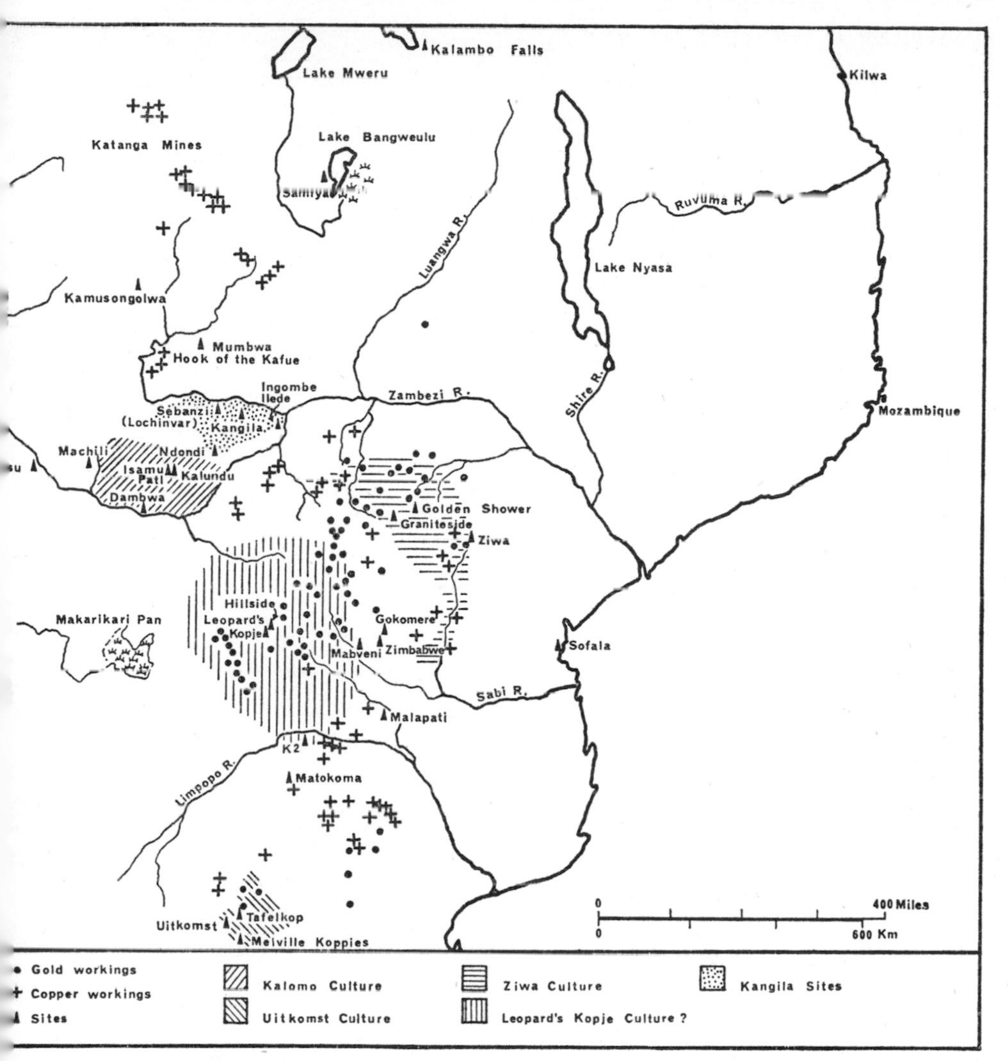

Fig. 16. Distribution of early Iron Age cultures and early workings in South Central Africa. Data from Fouché, 1937, and Summers, 1961

elements of the channel-decorated pottery tradition occur in the Dambwa assemblage. Some of the sherds bear grooved decoration which is indistinguishable from that on the pots from the earliest levels of the Kalomo culture mounds on the Batoka plateau, dated to the seventh century. Evidently Dambwa belongs to a period when changes were taking place if not in the population at least in the pottery tradition. Until further sites of this period have been investigated, however, we can say no more about the events of the time.

THE KALOMO CULTURE

Plate 13

North of Livingstone, the Kalahari sand gives place to ancient basement rocks, which form the gently undulating surface of the southern parts of the Batoka plateau. The plateau is covered with savannah woodland, but on the highest parts watershed grasslands flourish where trees cannot grow. During the last five years many early Iron Age sites of this type have been discovered in the Kalomo district and in the Middle Zambezi valley. These belong to a culture which has been named the Kalomo culture after the township of that name near which the type sites lie.

Fig. 16

Whilst the distribution of this culture is only imperfectly known, we have some idea of its geographical limits in the east. Kalomo culture sites have been found in the Middle Zambezi valley. Only two villages, one of them a fishing camp, are known from the south bank of the river, and none occurs on the Rhodesian plateau. No traces of these people have been located more than 8 miles north of Choma or further west than Nanga Forest on the borders of Barotseland. It is likely, however, that Kalomo sites will be found to extend further westwards to the fringes of the Barotse plains. The focus of the culture appears to have been in the Kalomo/Choma region, on the grassland areas that form the summit of the plateau. There, the *Brachystegia/Julbernardia* savannah woodland gives way to watershed grassland areas, which, whilst badly drained, were suitable for occupation by agricultural peoples whose material culture did not permit them to clear large woodland gardens. These grasslands abounded in game, supported good grazing grass, and were well watered. Any settlements in the open were still within easy reach of woodland, rich in wild vegetable foods. Ant-hills, areas of deeper soil on the watershed, and the fringes of the *Brachystegia* woodland permitted cultivation of sorghum, millet and minor crops.

The Kalomo peoples who lived on the watershed were careful in the selection of their village sites. They tended to live on traditional settlements, which soil analysis has told us were periodically abandoned and reoccupied, the villagers alternating between three or four villages. This preference for traditional sites has resulted in the accumulation of deep midden deposits and the formation of large mounds. Soil analysis has shown that the Kalomo mounds are composed of a mixture of granitic subsoil and some occupation debris. From these analyses it has been concluded that the occupants of the mounds systematically built up the village by quarrying subsoil in near-by pans, thus adding to the size of the mounds. No doubt the reasons for this were connected with drainage, cleanliness, and, perhaps, visibility and protection in an area abounding in predators.

Plate 14

Extensive excavations on two of these mounds, Isamu Pati and Kalundu, were carried out in 1957, 1960, 1961 and 1962, and our knowledge of the Kalomo culture people is derived very largely from them. The diggings revealed that the mounds were on an average 8 to 10 feet deep. Eight radiocarbon dates from Isamu Pati show that the heyday of the Kalomo culture was at the end of the first millennium. By means of an ingenious statistical analysis, Daniels has been able to demonstrate that the least improbable chronology for the Isamu Pati site is between AD 720 and 1200. The Kalundu mound is still undated, but the village is thought to have been founded at a slightly earlier date than that at Isamu, for grooved pottery found at the bottom of Kalundu is absent from the deposits of the dated village.

A long typological sequence of pottery has been recovered from the two excavations. In the lower levels of Kalundu, the

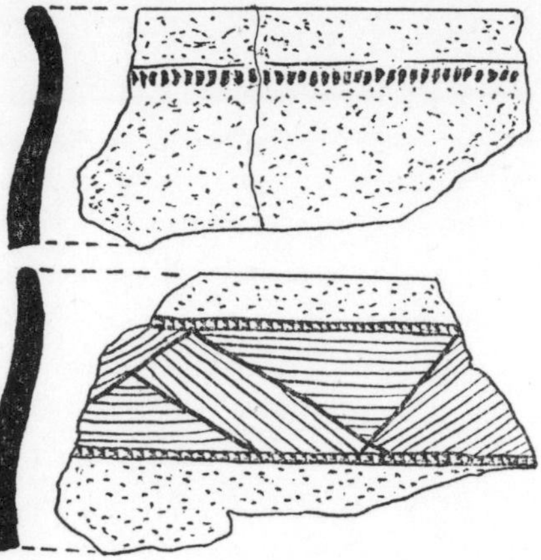

Fig. 17. Early Kalomo culture sherds from Kalundu mound. Similar vessels are found at Dambwa. 1 : 4

earliest mound known, grooved pottery is characteristic and is associated with shouldered pots bearing bands of comb-stamping. Spheroidal bowls with bands of similar decoration also occur. The earliest Kalomo culture pottery recalls some of the vessels from Dambwa. As Dambwa is considered to have affinities with channel-decorated wares, it would seem that some elements of the earlier traditions survived in the earliest Kalomo vessels. At the base of the Isamu Pati there is no grooved ware, but the sherds resemble the pottery in the lower levels at Kalundu. Indeed, grooved decoration and the other features reminiscent of channel-decorated wares vanish at this stage and are absent from the rest of the sequence. The characteristic forms are simple pots with rim bands decorated with cross-hatched, comb-stamped or incised bands. Graphite burnish is cunningly used to enhance the decorative effect; the pottery is of fine quality. In the final stages, the simple vessels are replaced by a sudden flood of globular pots, obviously designed for carrying liquids. There are, it seems, three stages of pottery development, of which only the first has parallels with earlier traditions. Such evidence is open to several interpretations. Either the Kalomo people are direct descendants of earlier

Fig. 17

Fig. 18

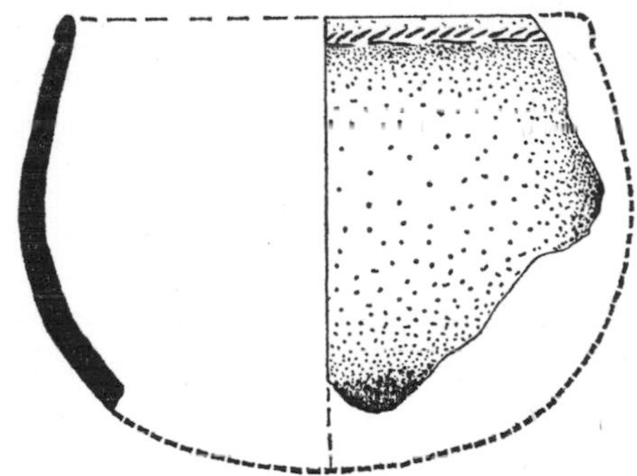

Fig. 18. A typical, later Kalomo culture pot from Isamu Pati. 1 : 4

peoples, in which case one would expect a longer survival of the earlier pottery traits; or they are immigrants who, upon arrival, absorbed some of the pottery tradition of their predecessors. Whatever happened, the old traits do not appear to have survived very long in the material culture, and it is more likely, to judge both from the typology of the pottery and from the distinct site distribution, that the Kalomo people were immigrants. Oral tradition collected by C. M. N. White in the Balovale district, far to the west of the Batoka plateau, speaks of migrations of Bantu-speakers into Barotseland in the late first millennium. It is possible that the Kalomo people were one of the early groups of Bantu-speaking people who moved from Angola and the Congo into Zambia. One must not, however, underestimate the contribution of earlier Iron Age peoples to the culture of the new immigrants.

Huts were made of mud and sticks, the daga being plastered on the inside of the walls. Roofs were probably the usual conical thatched type. Daga structures were rare, and it is probable that many of their houses and other structures were built of more flimsy and perishable materials, which do not survive in the archaeological record. Excavations at Isamu Pati showed that two groups of huts were separated by an open space which contained the remains of nine burials. Soil analysis has shown that the phosphate content of the deposits in the middle of the village is high. The central area was probably a cattle enclosure. No signs of fortification were found, and it seems that the site was surrounded with a thorn fence to deter predators from raiding herds.

Plate 12

Eleven skeletons have been found in the mound villages; they were buried in a crouched position with a few grave goods. One burial was more richly adorned, with ivory and iron bangles and shell beads, suggesting that the owner was a more important personality than the other individuals. There are Negroid elements in the skeletal material.

Fig. 19

Heavy iron tools are conspicuous by their absence, and the metalworkers spent much of their time turning out arrowheads, razors, bangles, and rings by simple techniques. A much worn hoe at Isamu Pati suggests that a few agricultural tools were made of iron and much treasured; they were only abandoned when no longer of use. Wooden digging-sticks weighted with bored stones were used for grubbing for insects and wild tubers, and may have also served for use in the gardens. The lack of iron cutting tools must have been a severe handicap to their agricultural activities.

The Kalomo mound people seem to have depended on local sources for most of their requirements, for their plateau homeland was isolated from the trade routes of the Zambezi and Rhodesia by the great escarpments of the Gwembe valley. Isolated finds of sea-shells, glass beads and copper objects testify to occasional trade with villages situated near the Zambezi trade routes and outcrops of minerals.

The economy of the mound people was probably typical of Iron Age peoples of the period. Carbonized seeds of sorghum were found in the mounds and, in all probability, millet and a number of less important crops were cultivated as well. As

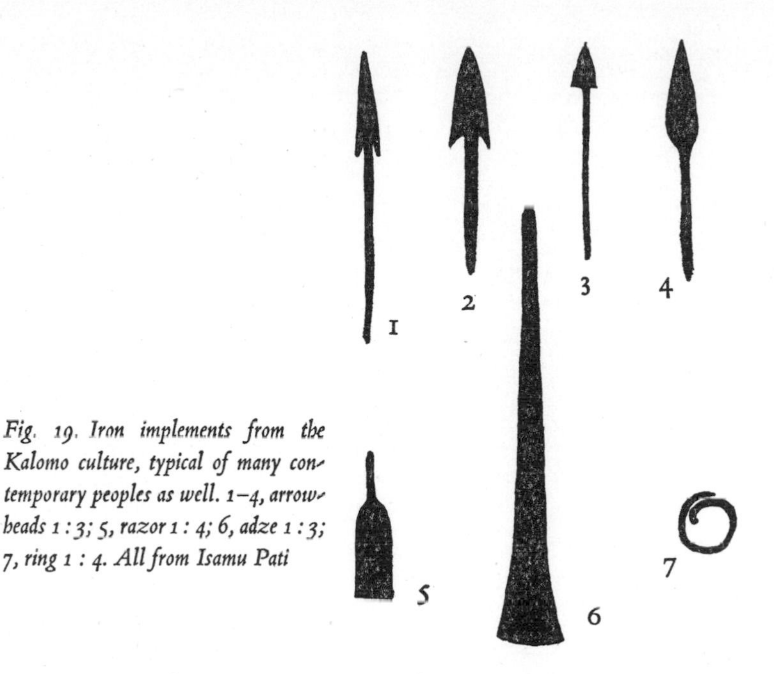

Fig. 19. Iron implements from the Kalomo culture, typical of many contemporary peoples as well. 1–4, arrowheads 1 : 3; 5, razor 1 : 4; 6, adze 1 : 3; 7, ring 1 : 4. All from Isamu Pati

with most African tribes today, it is probable that a porridge made from cereal crops formed the basic staple diet, meat and wild produce being eaten with the porridge as a relish. Wild produce played an important part in Kalomo diet. The fruit of the fig, musuku and other bush trees were eaten and wild vegetables were made into relish. Sanga shorthorn cattle and small livestock were kept; the mortality curves reconstructed from their jaws showing that they were slaughtered in their prime for meat. Dogs roamed the villages and were used for hunting. A wide variety of game was hunted; noticeably the smaller species of antelope, duiker, oribi, steenbok, reed-buck, impala and bush pig were frequently taken. More rarely, the Kalomo people killed eland, hartebeest and roan. The skill of the hunters, who must have taken advantage of the habits of their prey, is shown by the preponderance of adult beasts. Tortoises, hares and small rodents, such as the pouched mouse and the cane rat, were trapped and eaten as well. The study of the bones in the mounds has shown that there was an increase in the amount of meat from domestic sources consumed in the later stages of the culture. This is, no doubt, a reflection of the improvement in herd output, rather than of any drastic change in economic practices.

Human figurines with scarified stomachs were made of clay, as were models of cattle and other animals. The human figures are quite unlike those from Rhodesian Early Iron Age sites, but must have played some part in Kalomo culture ritual.

The picture of this important Iron Age culture we obtain from the mound excavations is an accurate record of life in Zambia at the time. The significance of the Kalomo investigations lies in the light they throw on the life of subsistence farming communities in Southern Africa a thousand years ago.

THE KANGILA PEOPLE
Fig. 16

Although the Kalomo culture people settled a large tract of the Batoka plateau, they apparently did not penetrate the northern parts of the uplands. There, the highlands reach an altitude of about 4,000 feet, and the *Brachystegia/Julbernardia* woodland gives way to tracts of open *Acacia* grassland. In the east, the plateau is bounded by the steep Zambezi escarpment, but in the west the high ground descends gently to the southern edges of the Central Kafue basin. The Kafue River itself flows through a vast seasonally inundated flood-plain, which extends as far west as Namwala. The plain abounds with game, and its short grass is eminently suitable for cattle grazing. Early Iron Age settlements are found far to the west on the border of the Kafue National Park, and will probably be discovered even further westwards in future years.

An isolated find of channel-decorated sherds at Lochinvar has shown that early farming groups dwelt in this region, but we know little about them. The earliest farmers were succeeded by a later Iron Age people whose pottery distinguishes them from their Kalomo culture neighbours to the south.

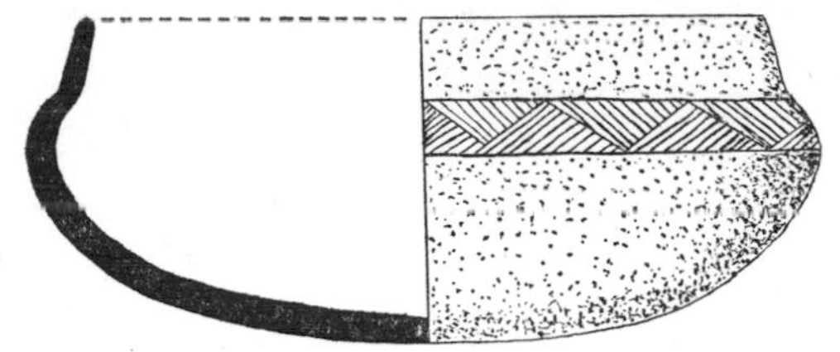

Fig. 20. Incised bowl from Kangila. Diameter at lip 6½ in.

The type site of these people, on Kangila farm in the Mazabuka district, was excavated in 1961, and similar sites are known from as far south as Ndondi near Pemba, with an isolated settlement in the Namwala district. No Kangila sites are found in the Middle Zambezi valley, although certain of the sherds from the base of the Ingombe Ilede settlement, described below, are similar to the pottery from Kangila.

No radiocarbon dates for Kangila sites have yet been processed, but the lower levels of the Ingombe date to the seventh or eighth centuries and sherds of Kangila type also occur at Sebanzi Hill on Lochinvar in levels which are later than AD 1200.

There is thus every indication that the Kangila people were occupying the northern parts of the Batoka plateau and some areas of the Middle Zambezi valley at the same time as the Kalomo culture was flourishing.

There is a distinct contrast between the Kangila sites and the Kalomo mounds. Typical Kangila deposits never exceed a depth of 5 feet, and most of them are considerably shallower. This implies that, in contrast to the Kalomo mound dwellers, they were not occupying their villages on a regular cyclic rotation. A settlement was occupied until the surrounding fields were exhausted and then abandoned for good. No doubt reasons for this were environmental, for there are not the impelling reasons for traditional village settlement as there are on the badly drained Kalomo/Choma watershed.

Fig. 20 The characteristic vessel forms of Kangila ware are straight-necked, shallow bowls with a distinct shoulder and simple pots. Almost invariably, the decoration consists of lightly incised designs, especially criss-cross bands or hatched alternating triangles. In the lowest level of the Kangila site and low in the *Fig. 28* Ingombe Ilede and Sebanzi sequences coarse, incised decoration occurs.

The vessel forms of Kangila ware are not found in the Kalomo culture, and the pottery stands in isolation at the moment, although straight-necked bowls do occur at Ingombe Ilede in the Gwembe.

Housing was rudimentary. Baked mud huts were built, albeit of a flimsy type. A hut at Kangila had walls internally plastered with daga. It is probable that structures of wood and grass were more commonly used.

As with the Kalomo sites, iron tools are rare and of the simplest types. Small arrowheads with simple, hammered blades were used; slag of any type is rare.

The economy of the Kangila people was based on agriculture, stock breeding and food gathering. Both cattle and small livestock were kept. Faunal analyses suggest that they were the predominant source of meat. Dogs were also present. Meat was also obtained from hunting, duiker, puku, oribi and reed-buck being eaten, as were small rodents. No doubt wild vegetables and fruit also accounted for a significant part of the diet. At Lochinvar, fish were eaten in Early Iron Age times; they are not found in the plateau sites.

In many respects the material culture and economy of the Kangila and Kalomo peoples closely resemble one another. Both peoples were dependent on cattle, hunting and food gathering for much of their diet. The pottery from the Kangila and Kalomo sites does not owe much to the channel-decorated ware tradition of the earliest farmers. We do not know enough yet about the Kangila people to be able to study their origin, but the differences between their pottery and that of their predecessors are such as to indicate that they were immigrants rather than the direct descendants of channel-decorated pottery makers.

Sebanzi Hill on Lochinvar was occupied for many centuries, the lowest levels dating to before *c.* AD 1200. A long pottery sequence serves to link the earliest occupants of the Hill with the modern Ila/Tonga peoples who live on the Batoka plateau and in the Gwembe valley.

KAMUSONGOLWA

A rock-shelter on Kamusongolwa Kopje near Kasempa in north-western Zambia was excavated by Daniels in 1963. Iron Age pottery, some iron hoes, an axehead, and a copper bar were found in the uppermost part of the deposits, overlying a Later Stone Age sequence. A radiocarbon sample at a depth of four inches was dated to AD 1150 ± 95, showing that the Kamusongolwa occupation is contemporary with the later stages of the Kalomo culture. The pottery is quite unlike that of the Kalomo people, with cord-impressed decoration and wedge-faced stamp motifs in common use. This distinct Upper Kafue-Eastern Lunga pottery tradition is contemporary with at least the later stages of the Kalomo culture.

Between AD 400 and 1200, the Iron Age peoples of the Zambian plateau lived in comparative isolation from the outside world. Copper was traded from village to village, but only rarely did the agents of coastal merchants reach the Kalomo or Kangila villages in the remote plateau interior away from the Zambezi valley. It was not until the rise of the great Congo kingdoms at the beginning of the second millennium AD that the rich mineral resources of the north were exploited to any great extent by their owners.

Chapter VI

Rhodesia: Leopard's Kopje and the Miners

South of the Zambezi, the earliest farmers had settled throughout Rhodesia, and had penetrated into the northern Transvaal and Bechuanaland by the ninth century. The pottery tradition of these people was, as we have seen, based on channelled and stamped decoration and a wide use of shouldered pots and bowls. A number of regional variants can be identified, amongst them that of the Ziwa people of the eastern districts, and the Gokomere tradition itself, found as late as AD 850 at Malapati on the Nuanetsi River. Many features of the Gokomere and Ziwa vessels are still found on modern Rhodesian pots, showing the important contribution that the earliest potting traditions made to modern African culture.

In Matabeleland, there are only a few Gokomere sites, but many more should be discovered when further research is carried out. Enough sites occur to show that the earliest farmers settled in the western parts of Rhodesia. No sites of this early period have yet been excavated in Matabeleland, but we can assume that Iron Age peoples began to occupy this area at much the same time as they moved into the centre and east of the country.

The Leopard's Kopje Culture

Whereas in Mashonaland the Gokomere and Ziwa peoples lived undisturbed for much of the first millennium, the Matabeleland farmers seem to have come into contact with new Iron Age communities during the same period.

A distinctive Iron Age culture, known as the Leopard's Kopje culture, has been identified by Robinson throughout Matabeleland, in parts of the Rhodesian Midlands, in Bechuanaland and in the Limpopo valley, South Africa.

Fig. 16

Although little stratigraphical evidence exists, it seems certain that most Leopard's Kopje pottery is later than Gokomere ware and its relatives. Few radiocarbon dates for the Leopard's Kopje occupation are yet available, but it seems probable that it is contemporary in part with the middle and later stages of the Kalomo culture (AD 900–1200). The early phases of the culture must date back several centuries earlier than 900, and it can be shown that some Leopard's Kopje communities are contemporary with the early fifteenth-century Shona settlement at Mapungubwe on the Limpopo, for sherds of Mapungubwe pottery have been found at the Hillside site and elsewhere. At the Khami Ruins near Bulawayo, Robinson has shown that the Leopard's Kopje culture underlies the main Ruin occupation of the eighteenth century. It has been suggested that these people survived until as late as the eighteenth century in Mashonaland, but the evidence is uncertain. The Leopard's Kopje culture was adopted by the bulk of the Iron Age people living in Matabeleland and parts of Bechuanaland and the northern Transvaal during the second millennium. It was, in fact, the common culture of the area before the time of both the Shona and Rozwi chiefs.

Leopard's Kopje villages were built either in well watered valleys, or on the crests of ridges, or amongst the rocky hills. Although no settlement has yet been recovered with the spade, the huts were probably erected around a central cattle pen. Sheltered areas amongst hills might be used, and the gaps between the protecting slopes filled by stone barriers. Village layout, indeed, followed the same trends as in Zambia. The average diameter of huts was between 10 and 12 feet, and they were made with stick walls, plastered with daga on the inside.

The roofs were thatched while earth that had been pounded flat served as a floor.

Excavations have shown that the material culture and economy of the Leopard's Kopje people was very similar to that of their Zambian contemporaries. The villagers used small furnaces, some with domed tops, to smelt iron ore; two examples have been found on Leopard's Kopje sites near Khami. Iron implements were confined to arrowheads and hoes with simple blades, sometimes with an ogee midrib. Beads and rings were also made of iron. Copper was not in common use, but some ornaments were made from it.

Figs. 21, 22

Clay figurines of both humans and animals were modelled, the former sometimes showing steatopygous characteristics.

The Leopard's Kopje people were mixed farmers. Hoes and grindstones testify to agricultural activity, but no carbonized seeds have been found. Their crops probably included both millet and sorghum. Cattle and small livestock were herded. We know almost nothing of the breeds, but the horn cores show that many of the cattle must have been shorthorns. As with other Early Iron Age groups, food gathering played an important part in the economy. Wild fruit, seeds and vegetables were gathered for the pot as vegetable relishes; many species of game animal were hunted, including buffalo, impala, zebra, duiker and other species. Presumably the importance of game meat was relative to the abundance of surplus meat from their herds.

The burial customs of the Leopard's Kopje peoples appear to have been similar to those of their Zambian neighbours. A crouched position was favoured, with sherds, and sometimes animal bones, buried with the body. The physical type of the Rhodesian Leopard's Kopje peoples is almost unknown but it must have varied considerably during the long history of the culture. In the earlier stages the Negroid elements were probably absorbed by the predominantly Khoisan indigenous

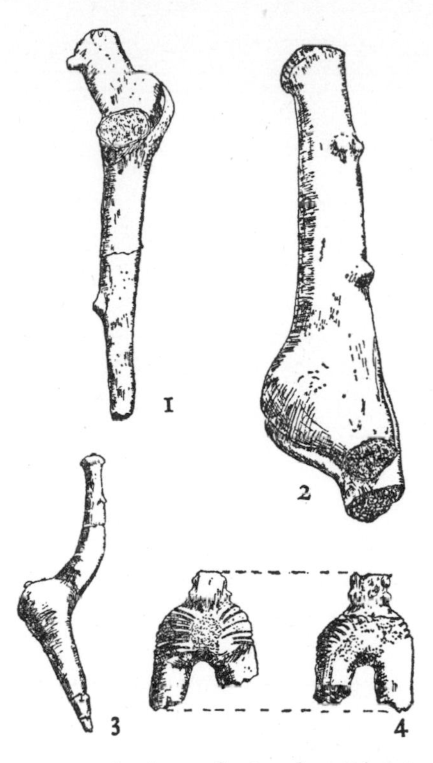

Fig. 21. Clay human figurines from Rhodesian sites. 1, Hillside; 2, Carleon Estate; 3, Leopard's Kopje Grave; 4, Mount Alice. 1 : 2. After Summers, 1957

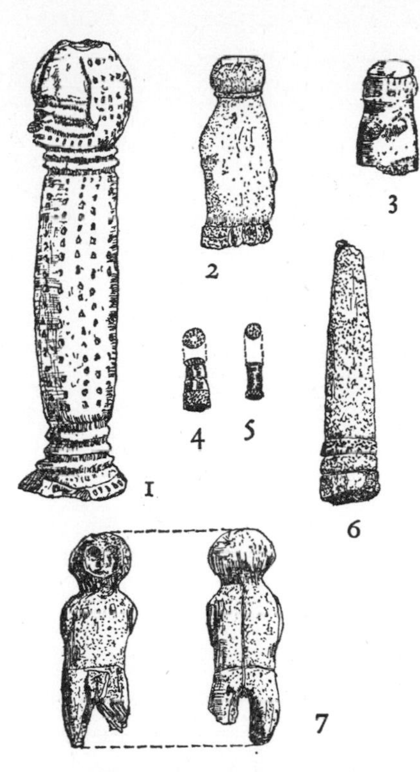

Fig. 22. Stylized figurines from Rhodesian sites. 1, Sipolilo; 2, 6, Zimbabwe; 3, Mushonga na Vhuri cave; 4, 5, Macardon claims; 7, Umtali Commonage. 1 : 2. After Summers, 1957

population, whereas in the closing stages of the culture the Negroid physical type must have become more dominant.

The salient features of Leopard's Kopje economy and material culture are very similar to those of other contemporary Iron Age cultures in Southern Africa in the late first millennium. The pottery, however, shows important differences from that of the Gokomere and Kalomo peoples. Leopard's Kopje pottery has only been described in outline. Unfortunately we

Figs. 23, 24

lack the long stratigraphical sequences characteristic of the Kalomo culture, and the full story of its development must await further fieldwork and excavation. Shouldered pots are characteristic of Leopard's Kopje sites, and they have straight or concave necks. These are normally decorated with bands of comb-stamping, meanders, or a line of chevrons. Deeper or sub-spherical bowls are plentiful, whilst shallow examples with incurved rims are also found. Beaker bowls and beakers occur, but are by no means abundant. Simple triangles and chevrons around the shoulder or neck and oblique rows of stamped impressions or incised lines are characteristic. At Hillside, considered to be a later site than Leopard's Kopje itself, a finer ware resembling Mapungubwe pottery is found in association with the native vessels. Such an influence is probably absent at the Khami Ruins where Gokomere features seem to persist. The presence of both earlier and contemporary traits from other pottery traditions is hardly surprising in such a widespread culture as this.

Robinson has recently subdivided the Leopard's Kopje pottery tradition into several distinct phases. In the earliest, Gokomere influences are strong. Coarse stamped decoration is

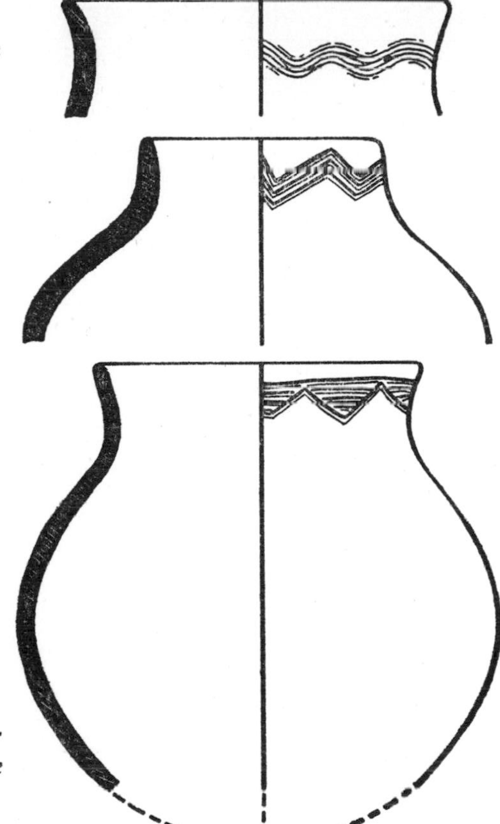

Fig. 23. Left, Leopard's Kopje sherds from Khami. 1 : 3. After Robinson, 1959

Fig. 24. Leopard's Kopje vessels from Hillside, Bulawayo. Collection: The Livingstone Museum. 1 : 4

found on many vessels. These traditional elements are combined with new types of pot such as the beaker, and the use of characteristic forms of incised decoration, which cannot be considered as part of the Gokomere tradition. Robinson suggests that in the south-western area of Rhodesia, the Gokomere peoples came into contact with Iron Age communities who were using beakers and decorating their vessels with incision rather than stamping. These beaker-users lived in amity, and intermarried with the Gokomere farmers, thereby giving rise to the Leopard's Kopje culture of the archaeological record.

In later times, the Gokomere influences in the pottery were gradually obliterated, and Shona traits are to be found, in the form of fine shallow bowls and delicately burnished pots. Some of the latest Leopard's Kopje pottery has much in common with the pottery from Mapungubwe Hill in the Limpopo valley, to which we shall return below. Undoubtedly, the Leopard's Kopje people came under strong influence from more powerful neighbours during the period of the expansion of the Shona and Rozwi empires, resulting in considerable changes in the pottery tradition.

Thus, the Leopard's Kopje culture of Matabeleland may have arisen as a result of contact between early Gokomere farmers and an unknown group of later immigrants to the western frontiers of Rhodesia.

The southernmost outposts of the Leopard's Kopje culture are to be found in the Middle Limpopo valley, where Gardner excavated the K2 site near Mapungubwe in 1935–40. The middle levels of this large midden have been radiocarbon dated to AD 1050 ± 65, and the pottery includes flat beakers and fine incised pottery typical of Leopard's Kopje settlements in southern Matabeleland. Such vessels are used today for catching

Figs. 25, 26

Fig. 25. Exotic vessels from K2 (Schofield's M2 ware). 1 : 9. After Fouché, 1937

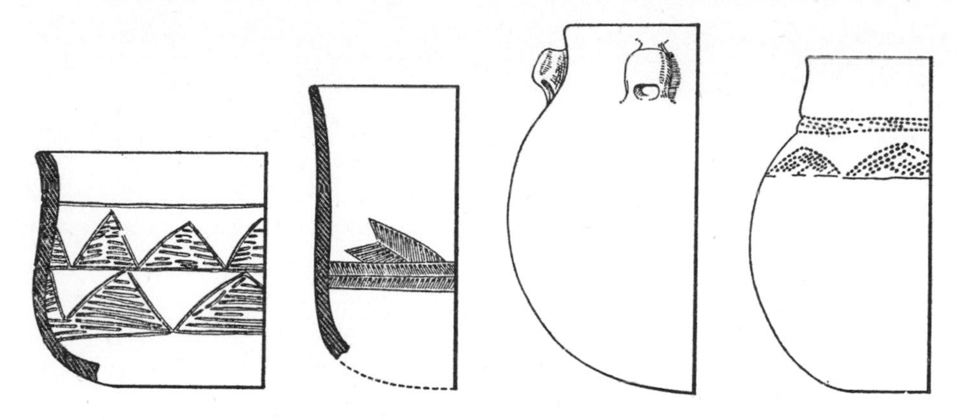

Fig. 26. Pottery from K2, South Africa (Schofield's M2 ware). 1 : 9. After Fouché, 1937

the dripping sap of the Malala palm which, when fermented, makes potent wine, and they are to be found most frequently in regions such as the Limpopo valley, where the Malala palm grows. The excavations showed that the village at K2 consisted of flimsy huts built around a central cattle enclosure.

The Leopard's Kopje people were probably one of several distinct Iron Age groups who inhabited Rhodesia at the end of the first millennium. In many parts of the country, the later indigenous peoples are still unrecognized, and await discovery by future generations of archaeologists. The subsistence farmers represented by the Leopard's Kopje people and other groups were the backbone of the Rhodesian Iron Age populations, for they controlled the mines of the gold and copper outcrops. They are unknown to us from ethnohistorical sources, except for a passing reference to tall, brown-skinned pastoralists, who were found in occupation of Rhodesia by the earliest Karanga clans to arrive from the north at the end of the first millennium.

In the Salisbury region, a number of sites have yielded stamped pottery, the most important of which is the site near Salisbury Kopje, excavated by Whitty. Not enough is known

Fig. 27 about the makers of this pottery to enable us to distinguish them from their contemporaries elsewhere in the country, but their pottery is sometimes referred to as Harare ware.

Another important site in the Salisbury region is the cemetery found during building operations at Graniteside and excavated by Boultbee and Goodall. A number of burials with Bush features were associated with large quantities of pottery, most of it undecorated. Until the material has been studied in detail, it is not possible to put this site in its correct perspective, but it has been radiocarbon dated to AD 1270 ± 60.

ANCIENT WORKINGS

Rhodesia is rich in mineral outcrops. Gold and copper ores abound; tin, lead, iron, and other metals can also be mined, often by simple methods and with unsophisticated tools. From the earliest centuries of the Iron Age the metalworkers of Rhodesia were not slow to extract the precious ores and use them for trade and domestic purposes.

Iron can be used for tools and weapons. Copper is easily made into ornaments which can be burnished and are not unduly heavy to wear in hot environments. Throughout the Iron Age, village bartered with village for supplies of iron tools and copper ornaments as well as for salt and other commodities. Such local trade is quite distinct from the large-scale commerce between the East Coast and the Rhodesian interior which developed greatly during the second millennium. Although the staple demand of the traders was for ivory, gold played an important part in the commercial network of the interior. The miners themselves do not appear to have made much use of gold for their own adornment, being content to pass it on to their more powerful neighbours and traders.

The Rhodesian mines straddle the Midlands, and extend to the west of Salisbury as far north as Lomagundi and into south-

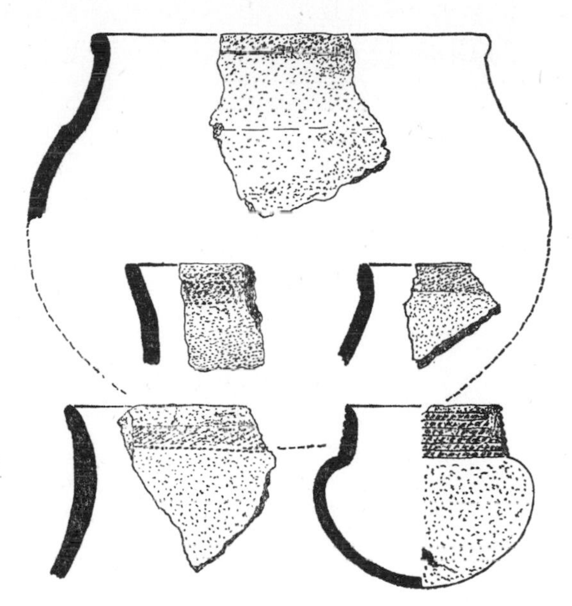

Fig. 27. Harare ware from Coronation Park, Salisbury. 1 : 4. After Whitty, 1958

western Matabeleland. Both gold and copper were mined. In later centuries, the Messina region of the northern Transvaal was an important source of copper. In addition, iron-mining areas are known from various parts of the country. Many of the ancient workings have been destroyed by twentieth-century mines, but it seems that open working was the most commonly used method. The workings were more or less V-shaped in section, with the footwall of the reef as one limb, and the extent of the mine was determined by the extent of the ore deemed workable by the miners. A trench, no wider than the reef, was first dug, but this was widened according to the dip of the strata. The work was carried as far down as the water table and ventilation would permit, but some workings go as deep as 150 feet below the surface. Rubble and rock would often be loosened by fire-setting, iron gads were also used to break out lumps of ore. Shaft workings have a more limited distribution in the north-east of the country. Only rarely were alluvial methods used. Few archaeological finds are made in the mines but the workers' iron gads, short bars of iron about the size of a

Fig. 16

cigar, are sometimes come by. These were resharpened many times before being discarded. Stone wedges and hammers, about the size of cricket balls, are also commonly found in open workings. Iron axes and hoes occur too, and a wooden bucket has been found in the mines.

The extracted ore was also selected visually and then crushed in stone mortars, after which the gold was concentrated by panning in a convenient stream. The dust was apparently stored in porcupine quills and traded, and it is possible that in certain areas a crude form of weighing was used to apportion the dust. Any ore with a yield of more than 3 ounces to the ton seems to have been regarded as worthy of further attention and the wastage by modern standards was enormous. Several young female skeletons have been found in the fillings of the ancient workings from which it would seem that much of the underground work was done by girls.

Mining was an essential part of the economy of these indigenous Iron Age peoples who were fortunate enough to live in proximity to mineral outcrops, and their quarrying played a vital part in the development of the Rhodesian gold trade.

The 7,000 or more ancient workings in Rhodesia are largely undated, although collections of potsherds have come from a number of mines. Human figurines have also been found. A number of imported objects, including a Roman coin of Antoninus Pius (AD 138–161), Indian brassware of the fourteenth and eighteenth centuries, and a sixteenth- to seventeenth-century ivory carving of Our Lady, of Colonial Portuguese workmanship, have come from early workings. It can be said that the mineral deposits of Rhodesia were exploited over a long period from the early centuries of the first millennium AD until the nineteenth century, when eye witness accounts of the mining are available. With such a wide chronological range for the mines, it is only to be expected that several different peoples worked the outcrops.

Sherds of early Leopard's Kopje ware, showing strong Gokomere affinities, have been found in prehistoric mines both in Matabeleland and the Midlands. Since no gold has ever been found on a Leopard's Kopje site, it has been suggested that these peoples did not use the metal themselves, but traded it with their more powerful neighbours. The archaeological evidence suggests that the first gold mines were started by the earliest Iron Age immigrants, presumably in response to a demand for the precious metal by pioneering traders from the East Coast. Certain mines in the east such as Golden Shower, near Arcturus in Mashonaland, were worked by Ziwa people, and there is abundant evidence that ancient workings were in use throughout the later phases of the Iron Age.

As far as we know, all mining activity was in the hands of the indigenous peoples of Rhodesia. The Karanga overlords who built the stone buildings of Mashonaland and Matabeleland did not mine the ores for themselves, but merely acted as agents for the coastal traders in search of metals, taking a share of the copper and gold for their own domestic uses.

Thus, the indigenous population of subsistence farmers and miners who first exploited the mineral outcrops of Rhodesia in the early centuries of the Iron Age, were vital to the thriving economy which developed with the arrival of the first Karanga peoples at the end of the first millennium AD.

CHAPTER VII

The Commercial Penetration of the Interior

SO FAR, WE HAVE CONSIDERED the Iron Age peoples of Southern Africa as a series of communities who functioned in isolation from the outside world. Many of the earliest subsistence farmers lived in environments where mineral resources abounded, but they did not make use of them except for their own limited domestic purposes. The time came when expanding commercial markets of the East Coast made themselves felt in the interior.

Since Greek and Roman times, the East Coast of Africa has been of commercial importance, first to the Mediterranean civilizations and later to the merchants of India and the Far East, as a result of the discovery of the Monsoon wind cycle by Hippalus in the fourth century AD. There is little archaeological evidence of the early traders from the Red Sea. Isolated finds of coins, most of them of doubtful provenance, have been found at a number of places on the Coast. A collection of coins ranging from Ptolemaic to early fourth-century Roman issues have been found at Port Durnford, suggesting that Mediterranean trade continued during this period. A Greek commercial handbook of about AD 100, known as the *Periplus of the Erythraean Sea*, describes the ports of the Somaliland coast and the East African littoral approximately as far south as the island of Zanzibar. The author of the *Periplus* makes no mention of black people living on the Coast, and we can conclude that Bantu-speaking Negroes had not yet arrived on the shores of the Indian Ocean. The Alexandrians of the second century had a useful sum of knowledge about the East Coast, which has come down to us in Ptolemy's *Geography*. Ptolemy adds little to the *Periplus* account, but makes vague references to Mount Kilimanjaro and the East African interior. Black people were, by this time, living in the extreme south of the area he describes, probably somewhere on the north Mozambique coast.

There follows a gap in our knowledge of the Coast from historical records until Masudi's work, written in the tenth century. Nor is there any reliable archaeological evidence. The period was a crucial one for the Coast, for the foundations of the pattern of trade for the following thousand years were firmly laid. By the beginning of the fifth century contacts between the Mediterranean markets and the Indian Ocean trade routes had faded, but the network of commerce within the confines of the Ocean continued to expand. Indian, Sumatran and Indonesian seafarers visited the Coast in search of ivory and other African materials.

Undoubtedly, the most important export from Africa to the East was ivory. African tusks are soft and particularly suitable for making the bracelets used in Hindu marriage ceremonies, as well as for other manufactures. Indian elephants are rarely hunted for their harder ivory, which is economically almost useless. As a result of an inexhaustible demand for African ivory, the East Coast trade achieved an element of stability, which was reflected by regular contacts with the peoples of the interior. Other exports included tortoise-shell, gold, iron and slaves. Black slaves became known throughout the coastal regions of the Indian Ocean during the late first millennium AD, but were not such an important commodity as the other exports. Eastern traders bartered cloth, glass beads, china, sea-shells and other luxuries in exchange for the merchandise of the Coast. During the second half of the first millennium, the markets expanded and Far Eastern plants such as the yam and banana were introduced to the African. The xylophone and out-rigger canoe also entered Africa from the ships of traders and were diffused over much of East and Central Africa by the

Bantu-speaking Negroids who were colonizing the Coast at this period. The extent of the Eastern trade along the Coast is unknown, but it is probable that most parts of the East Coast, as far south as southern Mozambique, were visited regularly, and Madagascar was colonized by the Indonesians during this period.

The earliest Arab colonists to visit and settle on the Coast are thought to have done so in about the eighth century, but for several centuries their numbers were small. Early Arab settlers are said to have founded Kilwa, off the Tanganyika Coast, and also to have discovered the gold trade of Sofala, at the mouth of the Zambezi, by the tenth century. Eventually, the Sofala trade was controlled from Kilwa and goods were transported there by sea, and, perhaps, by direct overland routes from Mashonaland. The heyday of Arab trading on the East Coast was from the middle of the thirteenth to the end of the fifteenth century, when the Portuguese arrived by the South African route. The Arabs did not penetrate to the interior of East Africa until fairly recent times, primarily because of the arid belt separating the Coast from the inland plateau, but the commercial exploitation of the interior of Southern Africa expanded when the Arabs came into direct contact with the peoples of the Mashonaland gold areas. Although most of the interior trade was conducted through black middlemen, an essential part of Arab policy was to place themselves in a position where they could exercise a subtle and persuasive influence on local rulers, to their own advantage. Such a policy was successfully used by Arab traders for several centuries in Rhodesia.

The routes traders used to pass into the interior from Sofala and the Mozambique coast are imperfectly known, but they probably followed highways which were, to a considerable extent, dictated by geographical factors. Great river valleys such as those of the Zambezi, Sabi and Limpopo were important gates to the inland plateaux. The tributaries of the Zambezi—the Mazoe, Shire, Luangwa and Kafue—provided methods of travelling to the plateau from the river. In addition, the valleys themselves abound in elephants and provide a ready source of ivory. To the ivory trader, the Zambezi was particularly important, because, for much of its length, the river is navigable by dugout canoe, a more economic method of carrying loads than the backs of slaves. By means of the river valleys and other natural highways, traders penetrated into the heart of Central Africa during the first millennium AD.

The evidence for early trading contacts in the interior comes from a number of early Iron Age sites on both sides of the Zambezi. Keith Robinson found a *conus* sea-shell in his excavations at the Gokomere rock-shelter, the type site of the Gokomere culture. This has been identified as *Conus hebraeus L.*, an East Coast species. Radiocarbon tests show the base of the level in which the shell was found to date from AD 530 ± 120. The burial with which the *conus* was associated came from the upper levels of the Gokomere culture horizon and may, therefore, date from the sixth or seventh centuries. Glass beads of the type which antedate the stone buildings at Zimbabwe were found in the same layer. Beads were also found at the Gokomere culture site known as Mabveni in the Chibi reserve, which is thought to be broadly contemporary with Gokomere itself.

North of the Zambezi, a single cowrie shell was found in the bedrock level of the Kalomo culture mound known as Kalundu. A slightly later horizon at Isamu Pati nearby has been dated to AD 650, suggesting that this shell was worn at Kalundu during the mid-seventh century or earlier. This find is important, for the Batoka highlands are well isolated from the main Zambezi trade route and there was little incentive for trading with the plateau peoples. A sea-shell in such an early context in this remote area indicates that the Zambezi trade must have become well established by this time.

INGOMBE ILEDE

Downstream of the Batoka Gorge, the Zambezi flows through a wide valley bounded by 2,000 foot escarpments. This valley, known as the Gwembe, is, or was, readily traversed by canoe, except for the length of the Kariba Gorge. It still abounds in elephants and is thought to have been the upstream limit of the Zambezi ivory trade for many centuries.

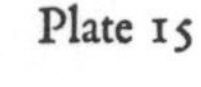

Plate 15

Plate 18

Some 32 miles downstream of the Kariba dam wall, near where the Lusitu stream joins the north bank of the Zambezi, a low ridge known as Ingombe Ilede ('The place where cows sleep') dominates the landscape for some distance. During 1960 human burials were found on the hill and J. H. Chaplin carried out a rescue dig on the Ingombe Ilede. He recovered the remains of eleven skeletons, some of them richly adorned with gold, copper and iron objects. In 1961 I returned to the Ingombe to carry out selective excavations to fill in the background to the burials, and recovered further undecorated burials in

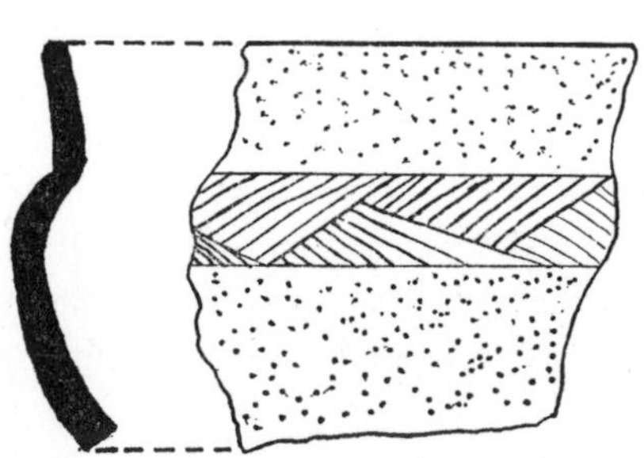

Fig. 28. Two sherds from the lower levels of Ingombe Ilede (cf. fig. 20). 1:3

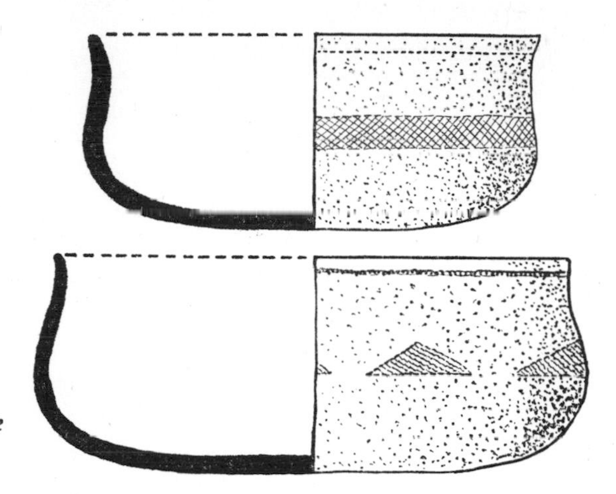

Fig. 29. Two fine bowls from the upper levels of Ingombe Ilede. 1 : 3

1962. The excavations at this important site have enabled us to catch a glimpse of the Zambezi trade about a thousand years ago. The deepest parts of the Ingombe Ilede are 8 feet deep and there were considerable changes in pottery and material culture throughout thc stratigraphical sequences. Radiocarbon tests have shown the lowest levels to date from about AD 680; they contain pottery which has some generalized resemblances to the Kangila ware of the Batoka plateau to the north. The same vessel shapes occur. Bands of hatched, incised decoration are found and zones of alternating triangles of fine incision were also used. Although the economy remains unchanged for the duration of occupation, elephant bones are common in the lowest levels of the site. It may be that the hill was first inhabited by a group of elephant hunters from the Batoka plateau.

Fig. 28

In the middle and later stages of the sequence finer vessels became more common. Shallow bowls with round, straight, or flared sides are usual and bear zones of filled triangles or bands of comb-stamping. Shouldered pots, often undecorated, are also frequent, but are generally coarser in finish. The pottery from the upper levels is some of the finest Iron Age ware known from Southern Africa. Fine bowls are found not only with the

Fig. 29

rich burials, but also as sherds in the occupation deposit, showing that they were in everyday use. Graphite burnishing is used to enhance decorative effects, and red haematite polish is not unknown. The changes in the stratigraphical sequence of pottery are gradual, and it is difficult to say whether the finer pottery is the result of gradual evolution or cultural innovation. Vessels in the closing stages show some Shona influence, which is absent in the lower levels, suggesting a degree of cultural contact or intermarriage between indigenous groups and Shona-speaking peoples. Radiocarbon dates from the burial area of the Ingombe Ilede show us that the closing stages of the site to which the gold burials belong date to the mid-ninth to tenth centuries. The Ingombe was thus occupied for a period of three hundred years or more.

The economy of the Ingombe Ilede people was somewhat similar to that of a modern Gwembe Tonga community. They cultivated sorghum and probably millet, kept cattle, goats and dogs. As in the Gwembe today, hunting and food gathering were also of importance, in a region liable to famine years. Our excavation revealed few traces of huts, but it is probable that the Ingombe people lived in wood and grass structures of the type used in the Gwembe to this day. Few traces of such buildings would be preserved in the archaeological record.

Coincident with the increase in finer pottery is a rise in the quantity of trade materials. Glass beads or metal objects are rare in the lower levels, but above five feet the number of glass beads and copper objects increases and, to judge from richly decorated burials, trading activities must have become more important. The central burials show us something of the range of trade goods at the Ingombe in its heyday. Here the deceased were dressed in several varieties of cotton cloth, some of which are thought to have been grown and spun locally, since pottery spindle whorls are common in the deposits. Arms and legs were encased in copper and iron wire bangles, which were

Plates 17, 18, 22

covered with several layers of cloth and, in one case, bark-cloth. Traces of cloth were preserved wherever the preservative effect of the adjacent copper bangles had been able to protect the fabric from decay. Round the necks and waists of the principal burials were strings of gold and glass beads. The gold beads were of several varieties. Twisted gold wire bangles were found at the elbows of the deceased in the richest burial, who also wore a necklace of nine *conus* shells, one of which had a back-plate of hammered gold. The glass beads tended to be rather monotonous, with red, blue and yellow types predominating. Copper crosses were found at the head or feet of four individuals, together with sheaves of rectangular-sectioned copper trade wire and several sets of wire-drawing tools, including hammers, tongs and draw-plates. The copper bangles worn by the Ingombe people were made on the site from wire imported for the purpose. Single, flange-welded gongs were also buried with two of the bodies. These ceremonial instruments, which are traditionally associated with authority, were probably not manufactured on the site; nor were the straight-sided ceremonial hoes that had also been found with the central burials.

Plates 17, 18

Plate 22

Compared with the central burials, which were obviously those of the principal inhabitants, the remaining skeletons recovered from the Ingombe were very poorly decorated. A few had small strings of glass or shell beads around their necks, but the majority were buried without any trace of decoration. More than sixty per cent of the Ingombe Ilede burials are of infants less than a year old. As the richest grave goods are only found with a few of the burials, it would seem that trade was controlled by a handful of individuals.

Plate 16

The archaeological finds show that gold, copper, cloth, sea-shells and beads were passing through the hands of the Ingombe people. To this list we can add ivory (for tusk fragments abound in the deposits), probably slaves and, perhaps, salt.

Plate 19

This commodity was of great value in the Iron Age and salt deposits near Lusitu were still being exploited in the nineteenth century.

With such a wide range of trade materials in their control, the importance of the chiefs at the Ingombe must have been considerable. They obtained their coastal imports from the Zambezi trade routes and were strategically placed to obtain ivory from hunters in the Gwembe or by their own efforts.

Mineral outcrops do not occur in the Lusitu region, so all metals except, perhaps, iron were imported. Since there is no evidence for gold working on the site, it seems probable that they imported their gold in the form of beads, ornaments, or dust. Copper was evidently acquired in two forms, as cross-shaped ingots and as wire. Spectrographic analysis of the metal has been undertaken, but it is difficult to say at this stage, when only a few analyses have been made, exactly where the copper came from. The form of the crosses recalls those found both in the Copperbelt regions of Zambia and at the Lomagundi mines, some 150 miles south of Lusitu in northern Mashonaland. There is speculation that the Ingombe copper came from the Lomagundi workings, although conclusive evidence on this point is lacking.

It is difficult to decide from the archaeological evidence exactly what role Ingombe Ilede played in the trading activities of the Zambezi valley. The concentration of trade goods in the hands of a few individuals suggests that the site was dominated by a group of powerful chiefs or traders. Whether they enslaved the local inhabitants or had merely achieved prominence amongst them, we cannot tell. The volume of trade cannot have been sufficient to make the role of middlemen a full-time one. It is probable that the leaders of the Ingombe Ilede achieved prosperity by virtue of their geographical position, which enabled them to maintain sporadic contact with the coastal trading routes. By their control of the Lusitu salt deposits and of one of the outlets of the ivory trade, they were able to spread the sphere of their influence over a wide area of the interior as well.

About a thousand years ago, as a consequence of increasing Arab control of trading activity, numbers of Arabs began to settle in Mashonaland. The ethnohistorian, D. P. Abraham, has estimated there were no fewer than ten thousand of them in Rhodesia by the start of the sixteenth century. The aspirations of the Arab traders had a profound effect on the events which led to the establishment of the empire of the Monomotapas.

The trade routes from the Zambian interior down to the Zambezi were probably not very busy, although the copper mines in the Hook of the Kafue are thought to have been worked at an early date. Luba miners in Katanga were operating as early as AD 900, but it is uncertain whether the Copperbelt workings were exploited so early. An overland route may have been maintained from Kilwa Island to the Katanga mines, but there are no literary or archaeological references to it. Much of the northern trade, probably insignificant by southern standards, was, at this time, channelled down the Zambezi.

Plate 21

The foundations for the more intensive commercial exploitation of the interior by the Arabs and Portuguese were laid in the later centuries of the first millennium, but the full potential of the gold and ivory trade was not realized until the Arabs made their substantial political assault on the Karanga chieftains from the twelfth century onwards. This we shall deal with in a later chapter.

Chapter VIII

Ruin Builders in Rhodesia

By about AD 1000, both Mashonaland and Matabele-land were populated by groups of subsistence farmers, in part the descendants of earlier Iron Age peoples, whilst others were immigrants. With the development of the coastal trade, this indigenous population began to exploit copper and gold deposits, thus providing the raw materials of Rhodesian commerce. This native Iron Age population was dominated in turn by a series of overlords who lived in large settlements, some of them associated with stone buildings.

Construction in stone was not a normal feature of the indigenous miners' culture, although some field walling for cattle kraals is known from Gokomere, Leopard's Kopje and Ziwa sites. Finds of gold, glass beads and other exotic objects are rare in their villages, but comparatively common in ruin deposits. There are strong indications that wealth and power were concentrated in the hands of the Ruin peoples, who handled the trading of the raw materials so laboriously mined by their less fortunate neighbours. The distribution of the ruins is shown in the map. The sites are scattered throughout Rhodesia, and extend into Bechuanaland, the northern Transvaal and Mozambique. None has been found north of the Zambezi and the distribution is connected, in some degree, to the occurrence of suitable building stone.

Fig. 30

The structure was of two basic types. Often platform walls were made for retaining daga structures. These can be seen on the Acropolis at Zimbabwe and at Khami Ruins. In addition, free-standing walls, sometimes of impressive size, were built, especially at Zimbabwe. The walls of the ruins are all built of dry stone and no mortar was used. In Mashonaland, the builders made use of a type of granite which exfoliates in

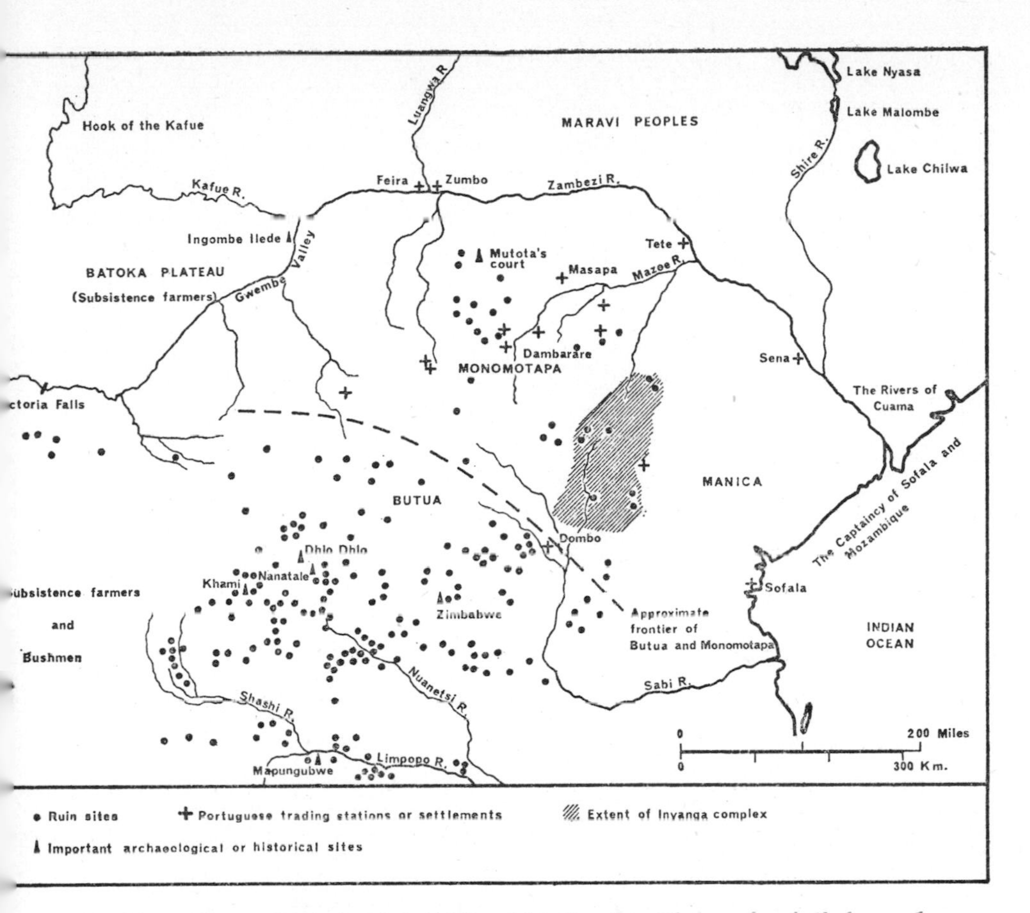

Fig. 30. Distribution of Ruins in Rhodesia (all periods). Data from Clark, 1958, and Abraham, 1961

natural layers about three to seven inches thick. The process was accelerated with fire and water. A central core of tabular, untrimmed boulders was enclosed by neat outer skins of coursed stonework. Straight unbonded vertical joints were left at points where walls intersect. Walls are almost invariably circular, and entrances are gently rounded with few right angles. The techniques of building are simple, but impressive. Whitty has worked out several subdivisions of wall facing and building technique as a result of his studies of Zimbabwe. It is not yet known how far these subdivisions can be extended to the other ruins, but they all occur elsewhere, even if their chronological relationships are not established. The Zimbabwe walls are of three types:

Fig. 31

'P' – The facing stones were not laid in even or level courses.

'Q' – The builders took full advantage of the properties of the stone and quarried it with greater care. The courses are regular and even. Chevron patterns were used.

'R' – This style is a degeneration of 'Q'. Earlier walls were robbed to build new walls.

It is noticeable that no buildings ancestral to these styles have yet been recognized. The Ruin stonework has peculiar features not found elsewhere. Furthermore, the distribution of stone buildings in Rhodesia is in no way connected to that in other areas in Africa, such as Ethiopia, where stone structures are found. This suggests that stone construction was adopted independently in Rhodesia, because of the suitability of the Rhodesian granite for wall construction.

The development and chronology of the Rhodesian Ruin culture is largely known from the excavations at Zimbabwe, Khami and Inyanga, which we shall consider at various stages.

ZIMBABWE

The Zimbabwe Ruins lie 17 miles south-east of the modern town of Fort Victoria. They cover some 60 acres of ground, dominated by a rocky kopje with a massive retaining wall, known since Bent's time as the 'Acropolis'.

Fig. 32

In the valley to the south of the Hill is a complex of ruined enclosures, the largest of which is the 'Great Enclosure' or 'Temple', with its high, free-standing, encircling wall, conical

Plates 23–30

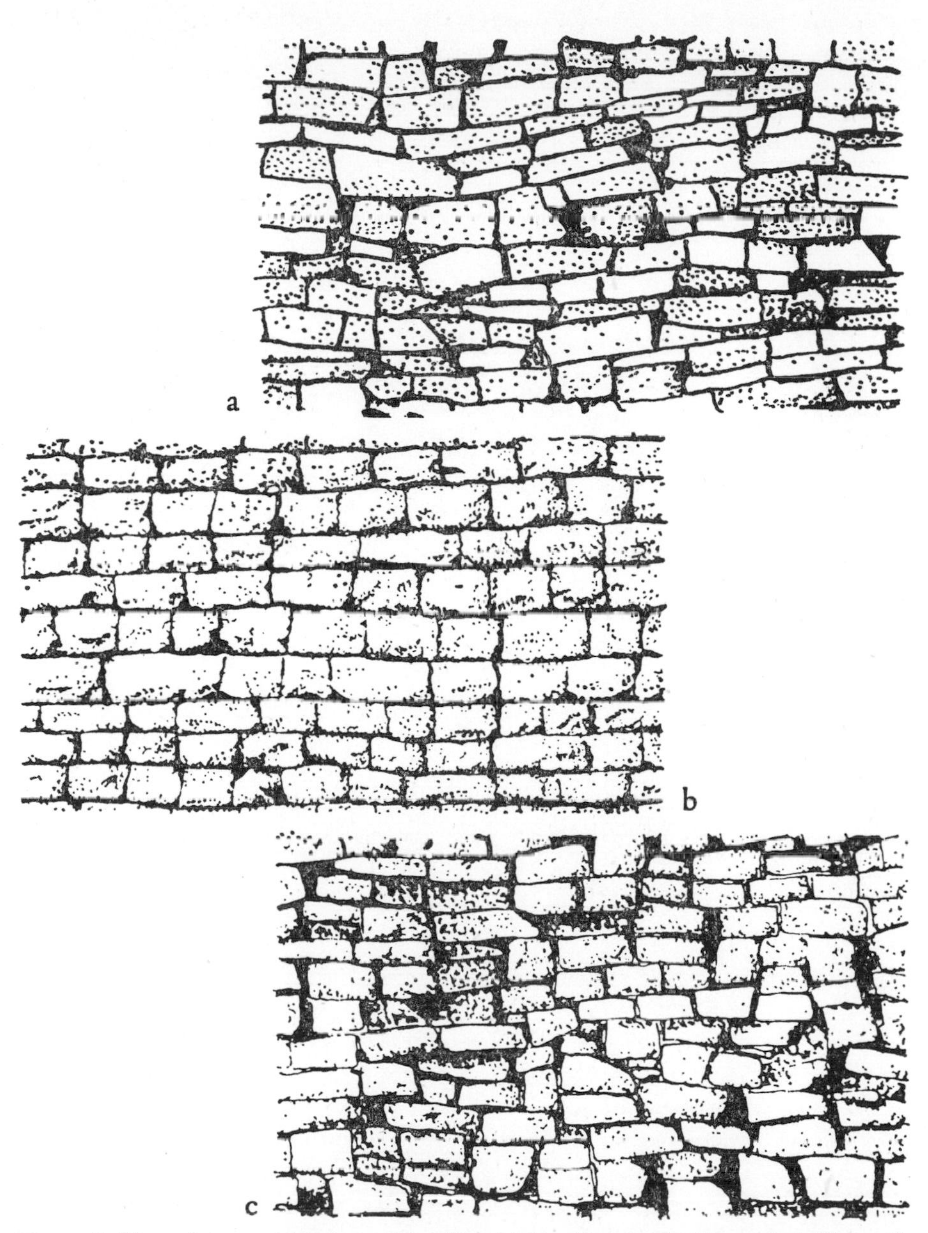

Fig. 31. Building techniques at Zimbabwe. a, 'P' walling; b, 'Q' walling; c, 'R' walling. After Whitty, 1961

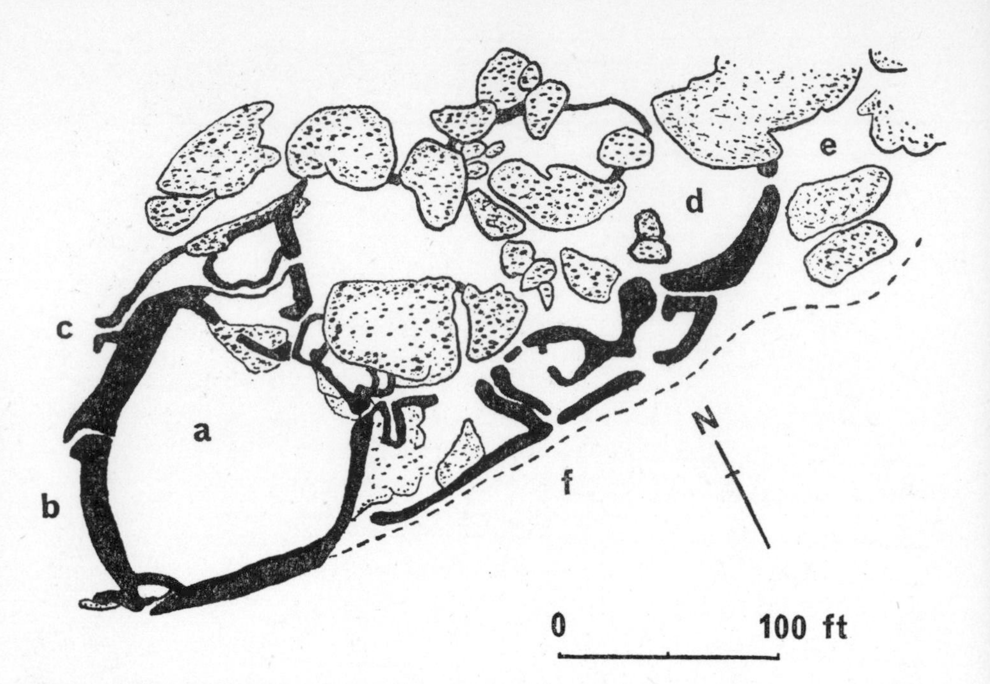

Fig. 32a. Plan of the Zimbabwe Ruins. The Acropolis: a. Western Enclosure; b. ancient ascent; c. modern ascent; d. Eastern Enclosure; e. Gold Furnace Enclosure; f. edge of 80-ft granite cliff

tower and other structures. To the north-west of the Temple lie other ruins—Renders, Mauch, Posselt and others. The Ruins indeed, can be divided into two interconnected complexes of buildings: those on the Hill, and the Valley sites. Zimbabwe lies on the edge of a gold-mining area, but there are hardly any ancient workings in its vicinity. The region remains green throughout the year owing to the frequent mists and rain which blow up the Mtelikwi valley, straight from the Indian Ocean, This isolated oasis of green in a comparatively dry area of the plateau must have been regarded as a favoured place by the occupants and revered as a centre for rain-making.

Plate 23

The Acropolis is a long, granite kopje, covered with enormous boulders. Successive generations of settlers linked them

Plate 24

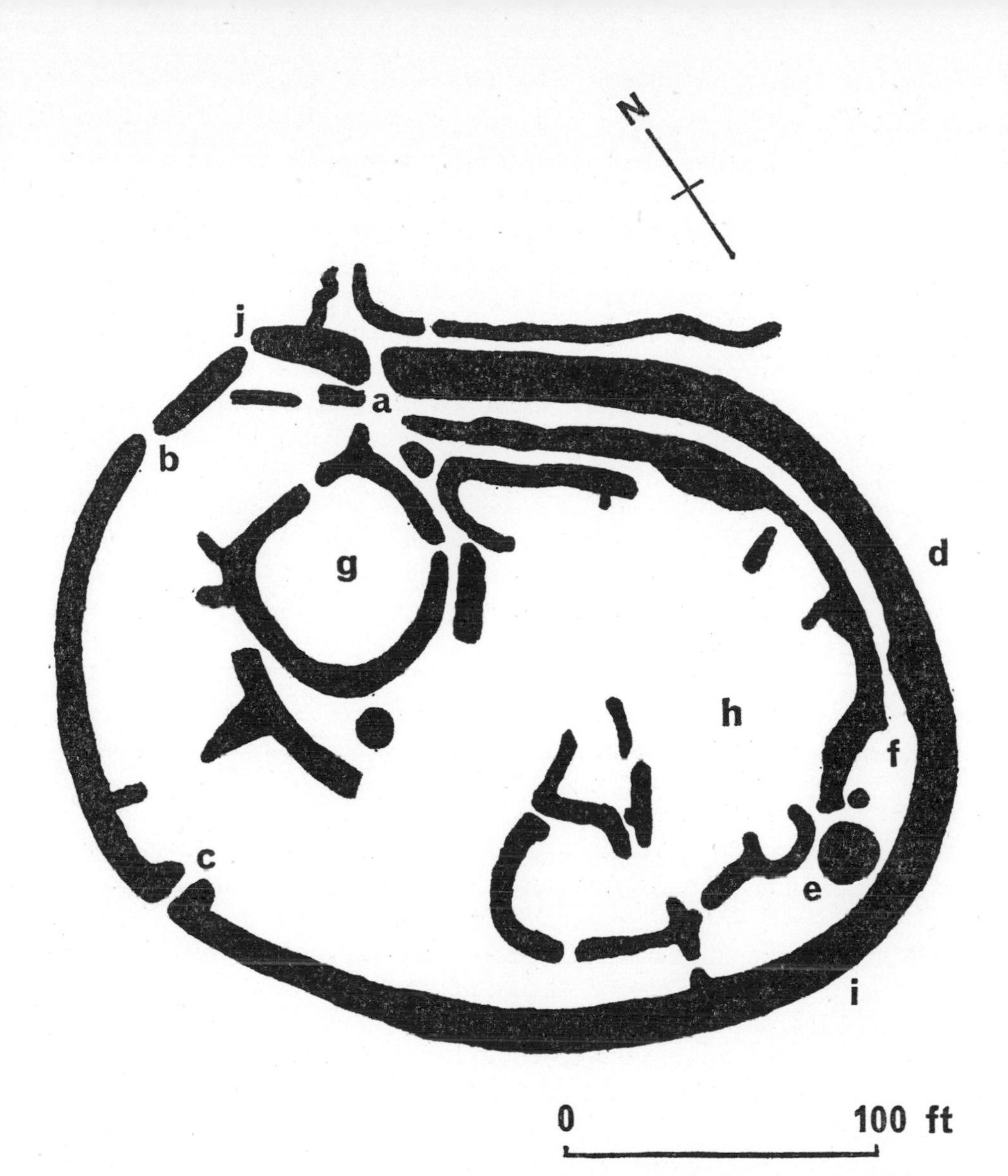

Fig. 32b. Plan of the Zimbabwe Ruins. The Temple or Great Enclosure: a. North Entrance; b. North West Entrance; c. West Entrance; d. Great Enclosure Wall; e. Conical Tower; f. parallel passage; g. an enclosure; h. area where traces of huts are to be seen; i. sector of Great Enclosure wall with chevron pattern; j. gap in the wall.
For the relation of the two ruins to each other, see Pl. 23. Plans from official Rhodesian Monuments Commission records

together into enclosures with stone walls and made passages. The eastern end of the Hill, now completely wrecked, was probably a place where sacred rites were performed, but the western parts of the Acropolis, known as the Western Enclosure, were occupied for a considerable period. Keith Robinson's excavations there in 1958 have given an outline of the history of Zimbabwe, which will provide a basis for all future work on the Rhodesian Ruins. He divides the occupation of Zimbabwe into five periods, of which only the first four need concern us here.

Plate 30

We have already described Period I, characterized by Gokomere pottery. The Acropolis was occupied by a group of early Iron Age subsistence farmers, who abandoned the Hill in the fourth century. They were the first incident in the long history of Zimbabwe.

After the Period I Gokomere people had left, there appears to have been a gap of unknown duration in the occupation. The hill earth containing Class 1 pottery is overlain by earthy midden and crumbled daga. The middens of Period II, which overlie the sterile layer, contain Robinson's Class 2 pottery. Although the date of commencement of Period II occupation is unknown, the closing stages of the phase are dated to the eleventh century (AD 1075 $\pm$ 150). Period II pottery consists, for the most part, of undecorated, gourd-shaped vessels, although some decoration of poor quality is found. Hemispherical bowls are also characteristic of this class of ware. Graphite burnishing is unknown and the pottery is of uneven quality and the firing erratic.

Fig. 33

Zimbabwe Class 2 pottery has been found at a number of sites elsewhere in Rhodesia. It is somewhat similar to the pottery from a site on Salisbury Kopje, and has been found on middens in the Chibi region south-west of Fort Victoria, as well as on some Inyanga Upland sites. The pottery from the late Leopard's Kopje site at Hillside near Bulawayo has some features in com-

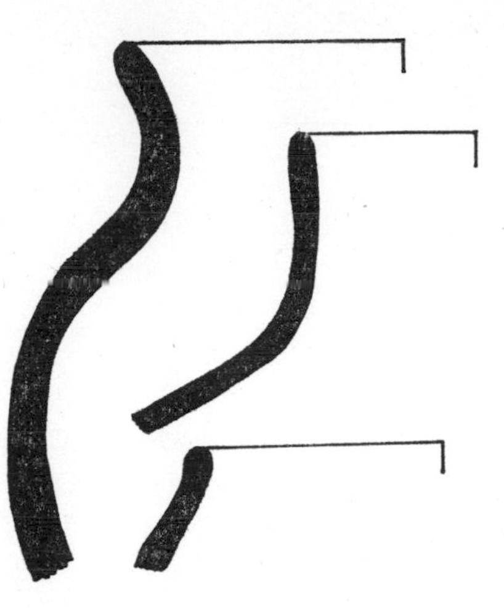

Fig. 33. Profiles of undecorated class 2 pots from Zimbabwe Acropolis. After Robinson, 1961

mon with Class 2 ware. It is evident that this pottery, which is a clear break from the Gokomere tradition, was, in various forms, widely distributed over Rhodesia. It may also be associated with mining sites. Robinson has shown that modern Karanga pottery is reminiscent of this ware, and indicates that Class 2 might well be ancestral to it. It belongs to a tradition which is widespread, varying slightly in form from place to place, and which is likely to have survived over a considerable period. Unfortunately, Zimbabwe Class 2 ware is the sort of pottery which is not readily identified in a fragmentary state and may often remain unrecognized.

The Period II people were also making stylized human figurines and realistic models of their cattle. A fine long-horned figure came from the Acropolis.

Fig. 34

No stone walls were built during this period and the tribesmen lived in thin-walled pole and daga huts of a type still made around Zimbabwe today. In addition to agriculture and stock breeding, the people were hunting game with bone and iron-tipped arrows. Bone arrowheads are an unusual feature, but are commonly found on northern Transvaal and Rhodesian Iron Age sites. Perhaps they were used when metal was in short supply. A few imported glass beads appear in the middens.

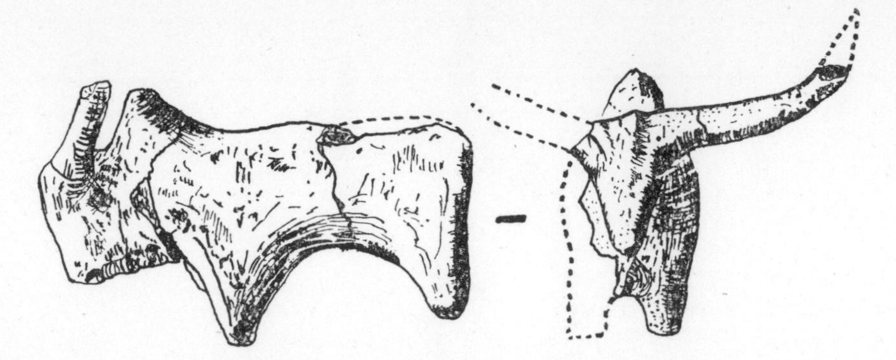

Fig. 34. Cattle figurine from Period II at Zimbabwe. 1 : 3. After Robinson, 1961

We are unable to suggest an origin for the Period II people or their relatives. As their pottery is quite unlike the Gokomere ware of the earliest agriculturalists, and has only vague resemblances to Leopard's Kopje ware, it may have been the work of immigrants. No Class 2 pottery is known from north of the Zambezi.

The deposits of Period II pass into those of Period III, which reached a thickness of 8 feet in Robinson's Test I in 1958. Radiocarbon tests show that this phase lasted from *c.* AD 1075 to 1440. There are profound changes in the stratigraphy, characterized by a series of substantial daga floors. The thin-walled huts of the Period II people were uprooted and thrown over the side of the Hill, and well-built and more substantial floors and huts erected in their place. These were, however, built alongside the older type of house in the earliest stages. Not only was a new system of building in daga introduced, but the ambitious work of constructing the south wall of the Hill from stone slabs was begun. This wall, and most of the stone work on the Acropolis, is classified as 'P' walling, indicating that 'P' style is the work of the Period III people, who specialized in building on rock foundations.

Further evidence for some continuity in the occupation of the Acropolis comes from the Class 3 pottery. The quality of the

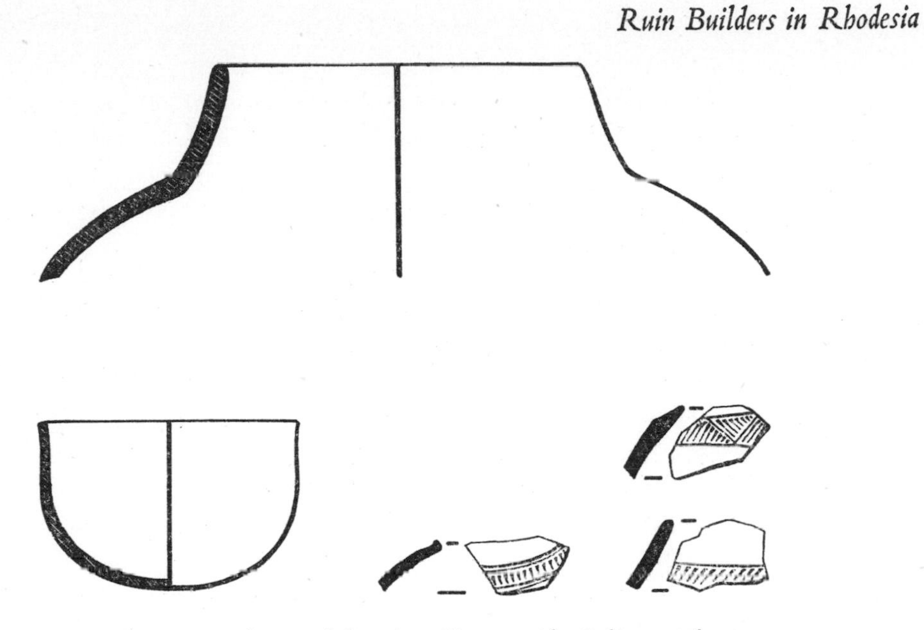

Fig. 35. Class 3 pottery from Zimbabwe Acropolis. 1 : 4. After Robinson, 1961

Fig. 35

potting improves, the clay is finer, and it is often given a high burnish, with rare use of graphite. Shouldered pots, many of them with vertical necks, are common, but bowls are now rare. Decoration is unusual but rows of incised triangles are found on some vessels. Class 2 gourd-shaped pots persist alongside the new forms. There is every indication that earlier potters continued their work under their new masters on the Acropolis.

There are other minor innovations. Spindle whorls are found for the first time, suggesting the wearing of fabrics. The glass beads are slightly different from those of Period II. Figurines are absent at this stage.

During this period, perhaps in the thirteenth or fourteenth centuries, the first buildings were constructed in the valley below the Acropolis. The earliest part of the Great Enclosure dates to the very end of Period III. This consisted of an area of daga, a large pit and a small enclosure, subsequently destroyed during later building operations. A fragment of Islamic glass of fourteenth-century date was found by Summers with this early structure.

Robinson has adduced evidence from the trenches on the Acropolis to suggest a phase of impoverishment at the end of this Period. This began with a series of hut conflagrations and may, perhaps, indicate a state of weakness at Zimbabwe, which was the forerunner of further change.

There is general agreement that the innovations of Period III were introduced by immigrants who may have been the predecessors of the present Shona-speaking peoples. The term Shona was first applied to the tribes of Mashonaland by the Europeans who followed them. Cultural and linguistic affinities seem to demand a blanket term to cover the tribes who inhabited Mashonaland before the nineteenth century. Karanga has been suggested as a more accurate term, and can be used as an alternative to Shona.

The material culture of Period III at Zimbabwe shows a degree of continuity with that of the earlier period, as if the immigrants arrived in small numbers and dominated the previous occupants of the Ruins. There is little information on the distribution of Period III sites or stone buildings, but the small Shona population must have spread over a wide area.

The origin of the Karanga or Shona is unknown, but they are thought to have Congo connections and to have moved southwards into Rhodesia during the late first millennium. No Shona sites are known from Zambia, although it is perhaps significant that the later pottery at the Ingombe Ilede shows Shona influence.

The Shona occupation is the longest to be preserved in the Acropolis deposits. It was followed by Period IV, which was the phase of greatest activity in the valley, and of almost continuous architectural developments in the Great Enclosure. The

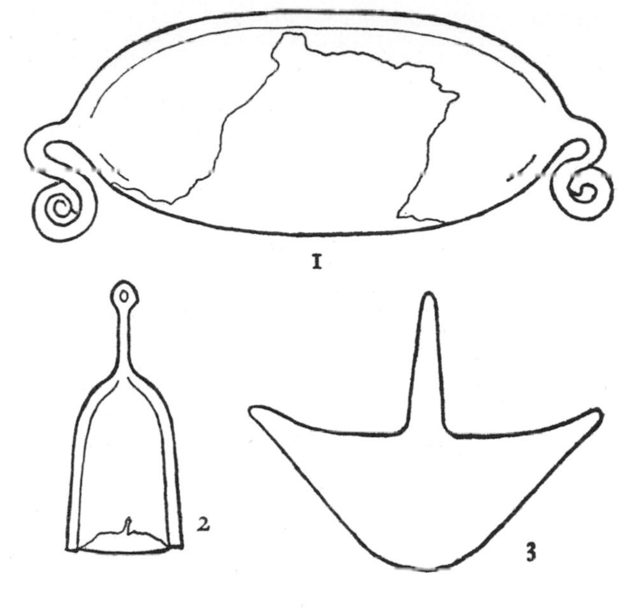

Fig. 36. Ceremonial iron implements from Zimbabwe. 1, 2, 4, gongs; 3, battle axe. 1 : 4. After Hall, 1905

phase of conflagration and impoverishment at the close of Period III is followed by a sudden enrichment of the deposits. Glass beads, china and other imports proliferate. Gold, copper and iron ornaments, iron tools and weapons, gongs, and copper ingots are found. Zimbabwe enters on its period of greatest prosperity. The pottery of this period, which dates from about 1440 until 1833, when Zwangendaba's Nguni destroyed Zimbabwe, can definitely be ascribed to the Rozwi. Class 4 pottery is typified by globular pots with tall necks. Spherical pots are found, which are characteristic of other Rozwi Ruins. Polychrome band and panel ware is also typical of Rozwi pottery, but it is rare at Zimbabwe, where it probably occurs in

Fig. 36
Fig. 37

Figs. 40, 41

a later context. It is, however, common at Khami and elsewhere.

There was vigorous stone building during the Rozwi period. Summers and Whitty were able to distinguish no fewer than eight stages of development in the Great Enclosure alone. 'Q' style walling is characteristic, a style which implies the most careful control over both quarrying and construction work. The highest level of technical skill in wall building was achieved early in Period IV, but the full development of architectural forms in which 'Q' walling was employed was not until late in the Rozwi occupation, between the sixteenth and nineteenth centuries. At this time, the Great Wall, the Conical Tower and the Platform were built in the Temple.

Plates 25–27

The vast enclosing wall of the Great Enclosure is probably one of the most remarkable features of the Ruins. Eight hundred feet long, the Great Wall has an average height of 24 feet and a maximum of 32 feet. It is as thick as 17 feet at the base, and is between 11 and 4 feet at the top. There are three deliberate entrances in the Wall, which were probably roofed with wooden lintels. The Wall was probably built to its full height on one side of the North Entrance before work had begun on the other. The general trend of the construction was in a clockwise direction from the North Entrance, gradually deteriorating in quality. The upper part of the exterior face of the Wall is decorated, over a length of the 168 feet on its east side, with a double chevron pattern in stone. We have no idea of the significance of the pattern-work, but chevron-work is widespread and may be connected with some form of Chieftainship. There is a gap in the wall where it was apparently intended to lean the two ends of the Wall against each other in the usual Zimbabwe fashion, but the circle was never completed. There is every reason to suppose that for the building of the wall a horizontal building technique, the general practice for Zimbabwe walling, was used. No post holes or traces of scaffolding were found, and the

Plate 25

Plate 27

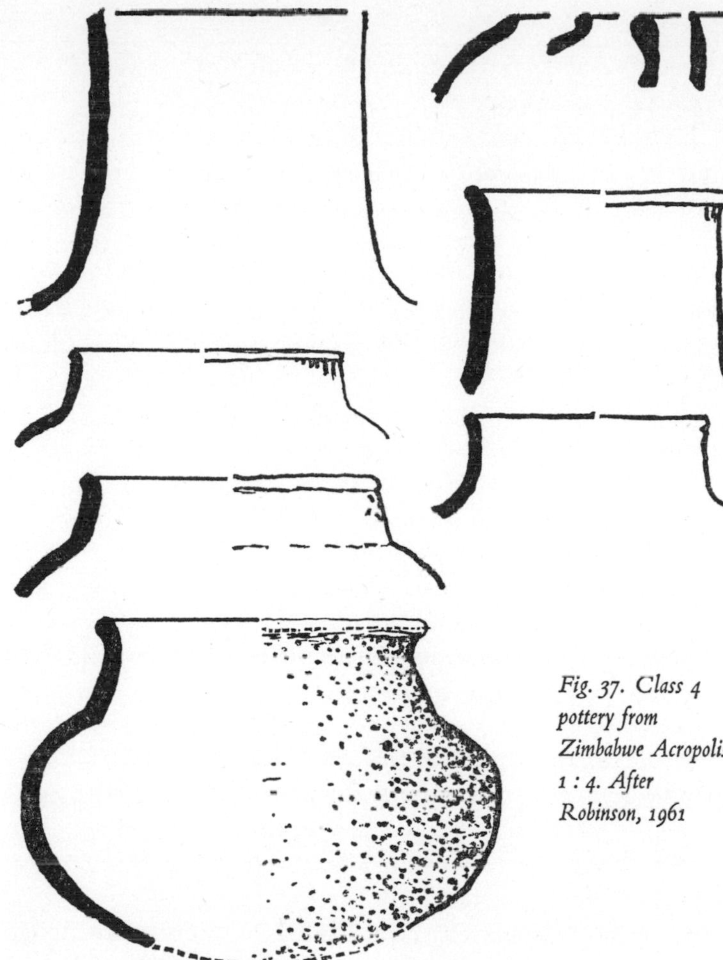

Fig. 37. Class 4 pottery from Zimbabwe Acropolis. 1 : 4. After Robinson, 1961

Wall was probably built as a gradually extending ramp, the porters bringing building materials up the slope of the unfinished wall.

The Conical Tower, which dominates the southern side of the Temple, is a solid structure and represents the finest technical and architectural achievement of the Ruin builders. The courses are level and even and the structure has carefully

Plate 26

battered sides, indicating skilful construction technique. Its significance is unknown.

The skill of the Rozwi in stone building was combined with other technological skills. Fine soapstone vessels were carved with figures of cattle, reptiles and other animals or with chevron patterns. Guilloche ornament was also used. Eight soapstone bird figures have come from the Ruins; all formed the topmost parts of pillars some 5 feet high. The figures were mostly found in the Eastern Enclosure on the Acropolis, an area where many soapstone phalli and bowls were found. Most of the birds have a long neck, a horizontal beak and feathered legs, the pillars bearing different symbols to distinguish the one from the other. These figures are considered by various authorities to represent either hawks, crowned hornbills or black eagles. Three of the birds are of a different, unidentifiable species. No records of the significance of the birds in Rozwi ritual have survived, but they are thought to have figured in some form of ancestor rites or rain-making ceremonies, such as are practised by the Venda of the northern Transvaal to this day.

Plate 28

Plate 29

Hut building in daga was a fine art. During his work in the Temple, Summers was able to reconstruct a sequence of daga types to aid him in the study of the history of the Great Enclosure. There were only minor changes in the style of building, but the quality was excellent. Rudimentary foundations were laid and drains constructed.

The most striking feature of the Rozwi occupation is the proliferation of exotic objects, indicating intensive trading activity and contact with foreign traders. Historical records for this trade exist and we shall study the history of the Rozwi occupation of Rhodesia in a succeeding chapter.

The occupation of Zimbabwe by the Rozwi *Mambos* or chiefs came to an end with the Nguni invasion of Rhodesia about 1830. A branch of the Ngoni under Chief Zwangendaba Kumalo ravaged Mashonaland between 1830 and 1834, smashing the power of the Rozwi chiefs and sacking their stone buildings. There is abundant evidence of destruction and pillage in the Temple, which presumably was the result of Zwangendaba's activities. Although the Rozwi may have continued to live at the Ruins for some years afterwards, Zimbabwe was occupied by a group under Chief Mugabe during the nineteenth century. He was related to the Rozwi and his people were still in possession of the Ruins in 1868.

The history of Zimbabwe extends over the whole span of the Rhodesian Iron Age, and it is a key site to which all other localities must be compared. But why was it so important? We have already commented on the favourable environment of the Zimbabwe region. The rocky summit of the Acropolis dominates the surrounding countryside. This impressive hill with its mighty boulders and caves became a focal point for ritual activities, perhaps connected with an ancestor cult having its origin in the earliest activities of the Iron Age. The ancient practices may have become connected with the cult of *Mwari*, the Shona monotheistic religion, which played an important role in the community life of Zimbabwe's inhabitants. It is clear from the accounts of Mauch and other early European visitors that the Eastern Enclosure on the Acropolis was a religious centre of great importance. Though detailed descriptions of them have not survived, gold burials were undoubtedly found there by the early investigators. The hidden passages and complex ascent of the Acropolis made it an ideal dwelling for the great *Mambo*, or the chief medium of the *Mwari* cult. Access to the Hill was probably restricted to a select few, the dwellings of ordinary people being down in the valley as were, presumably, the headquarters of the vast organization of which Zimbabwe and its Lords were the centre.

Having established the broad Zimbabwe sequence, we can now consider the history of the earlier phases of the Ruin cultures in broader outline.

MAPUNGUBWE AND THE SHONA EMPIRE

Period III Ruins, of Shona workmanship, are not common; some small ones occur in the south-east of Rhodesia. We have the impression that the population of overlords was a smaller one than that in Rozwi times, but their importance must have been considerable, for the volume of trade which passed through their hands was enormous. This can be appreciated by finds at Zimbabwe, and more especially in the middle reaches of the Limpopo valley. The Messina region of the Limpopo basin is rich in deposits of copper ore, which have been mined for at least a thousand years. Archaeological discoveries have shown that the Limpopo valley was the southernmost province of the Shona empire. The Hill known as Mapungubwe (The Place of the Jackals) lies a mile south and east of the confluence between the Limpopo and Shashi rivers. Mapungubwe stands out amongst the low hills and flood-plain of the Limpopo valley by reason of its flat top and precipitous cliffs, more than 200 feet high, and was excavated between 1934 and 1940. The successive excavators demonstrated that the occupation of K2 took place before that of the Hill. K2 pottery, named by Schofield M2, serves to link the site with Leopard's Kopje culture peoples in Rhodesia, and many of their culture traits can also be matched at K2. In the upper levels of K2 there are intrusive elements which may represent the first arrival of Shona peoples in the Limpopo basin. We cannot be sure until K2 pottery has been further studied, but it is certain that the last occupants of the earlier settlement were the first Iron Age group to live on Mapungubwe Hill. The lowest horizon on the Hill is separated from the next occupation by a layer of black ash. According to Gardner, with the black layer there is a complete break in the cultural sequence. Spindle whorls and abundant iron tools now make their appearance and the pottery becomes finer. The pottery of the main occupation, for the middle stages of which radiocarbon tests give a date between AD 1380 and 1420, is

Plate 31
Fig. 25
Fig. 38

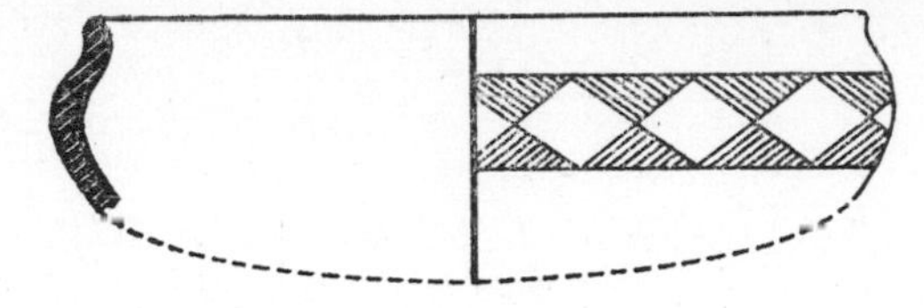

Fig. 38. Mapungubwe Hill pottery (Schofield's M1). Collection: The Livingstone Museum. 1 : 4

typified by numerous finely made shallow bowls, by beautiful incised decoration and a high quality of black burnish. The elaborate vessel forms and scratched decoration characteristic of K2 are absent. Schofield, who named this ware M1 and compared it to Shona pottery, showed that there were resemblances between M1 and the Ruin pottery of Zimbabwe. We now know that Class 3 pottery, made by the Period III Shona occupants of the Zimbabwe Acropolis, is closely similar to M1 ware, whereas Zimbabwe Class 2 pottery can be compared, in some respects, to the K2 vessels.

The excavators were able to show that both K2 and Shona pottery traditions were intermingled throughout the Hill deposits, but that the Shona ware became more common towards the end of the sequence.

The material culture of the Shona occupants was a rich one. Traces of complex daga structures were found by all investigators. These included houses with courtyards, huts with verandas and simpler structures. In several instances there was evidence of repeated rebuilding of the houses. The elaborate layout of the Hill structures suggests that they may have been for important personalities rather than common tribesmen.

Ironworking was practised, but no unusual ceremonial tools were made. Flat bladed arrowheads, spearheads, hoes and bangles were manufactured. Iron arrowheads were supplemented with bone points, some of them split to receive barbs. Clay figurines of animals were modelled, but human figurines are rarely found. Imported objects are numerous. Glass beads abounded in the Shona levels and are of the same general type as those found in the Shona deposits at Zimbabwe. Copper bangles and bracelets are common and were, perhaps, made on the Hill.

Gold objects are scattered in the deposits, but occur more especially with the eleven burials originally found in the western end of the Hill. Beads, bangles, and foil came from the caves. Gold tacks, used to fasten the foil to wooden objects, were also found. The deceased were buried in a contracted position, with the limbs encased in copper and iron bangles. The arms and neck of the principal burial were surrounded by great numbers of gold wire bangles.

There were traces of a gold-plated head rest under the skull. Nearby were a gold-plated wooden bowl, and the remains of a gold-tipped staff. Great quantities of gold and glass beads were recovered from around the remains of the skeleton.

The economy of Mapungubwe was based on the cultivation of cereal crops, herds of cattle and small stock. Although wild produce was collected, the inhabitants do not seem to have eaten much game meat.

This rich culture, which had its heyday in the fifteenth and sixteenth centuries, is known to us only from the excavations on the Hill itself. As at Zimbabwe, there are occupation deposits in the valley beneath Mapungubwe Hill. These have hardly been touched and may throw light on the political organization of Mapungubwe, for the pottery tradition survived alongside the M1 ware of the Shona peoples. There is every suggestion, from the archaeological evidence, that the earlier

Iron Age population was dominated by a Shona minority, whose influence on the material culture grew stronger the longer Mapungubwe was occupied. It will be remembered that the Shona peoples of the Zimbabwe Acropolis lived in amity with their Period II predecessors, although dominating them. There is, in fact, a striking similarity in the political situation at the two sites. At both, the indigenous population is dominated by Shona peoples whose culture shows that they were in close association both with the miners of copper and gold and with the organizers of the coastal trading caravans. Oral traditions speak of the importance of Mapungubwe Hill in ancient religious ceremonies and, even in 1933, Venda people were terrified of the place. Access to it and residence on the summit were restricted to a select few, the bulk of the Mapungubwe population living in the large village which was probably sited on the terrace to the south of the Hill.

The Shona were overrun by the Venda, who have strong connections with the Rozwi and live in the northern Transvaal to this day. Their polychrome pottery is not found on the Hill, but on open sites and in fortified hilltops elsewhere in the Limpopo valley. We know that the Rozwi arrived at Zimbabwe about AD 1500, and ethnohistorical evidence suggests that their Venda relatives crossed the Limpopo about a hundred years or more later.

Unfortunately, most of Period III and all of the earlier phases of Zimbabwe's history lie outside the range of historical records and reliable oral tradition, so we must rely almost wholly on archaeological evidence for the story of the Shona empire.

CHAPTER IX

The Empire of Monomotapa

THANKS TO THE WORK of Abraham and others, the history of the great confederacy of peoples who were ruled by the chiefs of Zimbabwe has been reconstructed, at least tentatively, from ethnohistorical and written sources. In its later stages, this traditional history is extremely complete, but we are only concerned with its broadest outlines, which can be related to the archaeological evidence from Zimbabwe, discussed in the last chapter.

Abraham has argued in several publications that the early Karanga or Shona entered Rhodesia about AD 850. They came from the north, their ultimate place of origin being the Lake Tanganyika region. They fanned out over the country, coming into contact with Bushmen groups and indigenous Iron Age peoples.

The new arrivals employed their predecessors as cattle herders and ironworkers. The population gradually increased, and the Karanga spread into the south and south-east of the country, towards the Limpopo valley. Armed with the mining knowledge of their more experienced neighbours, they located copper and gold deposits, producing ornaments for their own use. Their material culture was enriched and they progressively abandoned the crude domestic wares of their pastoral neighbours and developed more elegant styles of their own. In pursuit of their ancestor cult, the Karanga established shrines, the principal one on a hill called Mhanwa. This was named *Dzimba dzemabwe* (Houses of stone), and became the focal point of the nation, as well as the dwelling-place of the principal leader of the Rozwi people. By astute political manoeuvring, the first leader established an overlordship over a loose confederacy of vassal chieftains, who paid him tribute in ivory and gold dust. Arab traders on the East Coast, attracted by rumours of a powerful and rich kingdom in the interior, penetrated into the Karanga territory by means of the Buzi and Sabi valleys, and bartered cloth and beads with the leading families in exchange for gold dust and ivory.

During the thirteenth century, the Karanga came under pressure from Bechuanaland peoples, who began infiltrating into their territory, owing to the increasing aridity of the Kalahari Desert. The threat was met by the leaders of the Karanga, who organized their nation on a more military basis and, in the process, consolidated their own position of authority. All the doings of the Karanga were controlled through the king, who maintained careful control of the *Mwari* cult and ruled by means of a council of prominent citizens and by strategically placed regiments of warriors. It is at this point, the beginning of the fifteenth century, that individual chiefs and events begin to enter the picture.

An understanding of Shona religion is vital to those who study the history of the Shona and Rozwi empires, for these peoples' beliefs had a profound effect on their social and political organization.

Throughout the areas where Bantu languages are spoken there are basic similarities both in the structure of the grammar and the vocabulary. In a similar way, there are clear resemblances between the religious practices of Bantu-speaking tribes living as far apart as the northern Transvaal and Tanganyika. Shona religious beliefs are, like those of other African religions, closely identified with the spirits of ancestors, who provide a means of communication with a supreme being. This supreme being is believed to have been the creator of the world and of man. The Shona divine being goes under several different names, the most common of which is *Mwari*, a name which may be derived from the term *Muri* meaning 'you are'.

No living man can intercede with *Mwari* except through intermediaries. The Shona believe that the spirit of a man can speak with the Creator after death, and for this reason a system of spirit worship has evolved. When someone wishes to ask a favour of *Mwari* or to seek his protection, he prays through his own ancestral spirits. Such family spirits are known as *vadzimu* (sing. *mudzimu*), and whenever a direct relative dies, the spirit of that individual joins the family ancestral ghosts.

Mwari is also worshipped at the tribal level. The tribal spirits, or *mhondoro*, are the means by which the whole community or its representatives can intercede with *Mwari* in time of trouble, or when crops fail. Much of the ceremonial life of Shona peoples is connected with the worship and honour of *Mwari* through the *mhondoro*.

Both *vadzimu* and *mhondoro* are thought to express themselves through a medium, known as *svikiro*. The host may either be a member of the family to whom the *vadzimu* belong, or, in the case of the tribe as a whole, any member of the community may act as such.

The cult of *Mwari* is essentially a religion of the people. Since the living can only communcate with *Mwari* by way of ancestral spirits, the Shona show considerable respect and concern for the tribal elders and the older members of their families. Undoubtedly this respect for older people is a precaution to make sure that future *vadzimu* are friendly when the elders have died and joined the ranks of the spirits. Since the community can only contact *Mwari* through the hosts of such *vadzimu*, it is natural that the media through which the tribal spirits could be invoked were treated with extraordinary respect.

Everything points to the power of the Shona and Rozwi chiefs having been based on their intermediary powers, or on their control of the hosts of the powerful *mhondoro*, upon whose messages to *Mwari* depended the fortune of the community.

Before considering the events of the later centuries, it should be seen how the archaeological evidence fits into the historical accounts.

Period II at Zimbabwe, which it will be remembered begins sometime during the middle of the first millennium AD, brings with it a type of pottery which is a complete break in tradition with the Gokomere ware of the earliest occupation. Robinson has stated that Class 2 ware may be ancestral Karanga pottery. Period II, which sees the first imports arriving at Zimbabwe, ends about AD 1100. It is succeeded by a phase of intensive occupation by the Shona peoples of Period III. Class 3 pottery retains many features of Class 2, suggesting that some continuity in the occupation was maintained. There are signs of similar typological continuity between Periods III and IV, and there is a degree of similarity in the pottery of all the last three Periods.

That Periods II and III at Zimbabwe can be assigned to the Karanga Shona-speakers of historical tradition is not in doubt, but the exact identification of historical records with the archaeological sites cannot be made. It would seem, from the few radiocarbon dates which are available, that the chronology of the arrival of the Karanga and the commencement of Periods II and III at Zimbabwe agree in general outline.

Archaeological sites belonging to this dominant Shona culture are scattered over the Rhodesian plateau, but more field work is needed to fill gaps in the information.

Stratigraphical evidence from Matabeleland has shown that there was a dominant Iron Age Culture which pre-dated the Rozwi ruin sites of Khami and Dhlo-Dhlo. This imposed itself on the Leopard's Kopje people, who were the earlier inhabitants of the region. Later Leopard's Kopje sites have yielded new pot forms which display incised motifs rather than stamped decoration of the earlier vessels. Many features of this pottery are found in M1 ware at Mapungubwe, which, as has been seen, is in many respects similar to the Shona-inspired Class 3 ware at Zimbabwe. The beads from these sites also recall Period III. Period III buildings probably occur to the south-west of Zimbabwe and definitely in the Chibi region. Other sites may occur in the Sabi and Mount Darwin areas and in the Belingwe reserve, but the distribution is imperfectly known. Thus it was that what archaeologists call Period III in the Zimbabwe occupation, the great confederacy of Karanga peoples known as the 'Kingdom of Monomotapa', first came into being. The radiocarbon dates from the Hill at Mapungubwe suggest that the influence of the Karanga had spread to the Limpopo by the early fourteenth century. Oral tradition cited by Abraham, Fortune, Robinson and others indicates that there was a considerable movement of the principal families during Period III.

With the beginning of Period IV, about 1450, we emerge into clearer historical perspective. There can be little doubt that the basic material culture of the Period IV people is derived from that of Period III. The greatest phase of Zimbabwe's history is assigned to the Rozwi. There have been many explanations of the word 'Rozwi', but none of these is really satisfactory. The term does not appear to have been in daily use until the seventeenth century. They were probably a ruling clan of the Karanga who rose to power by reason of their political acumen and ritual powers. As the ruling clan, they kept themselves aloof from the common people. Tribute in the form of work, agricultural produce, cattle and trade materials was undoubtedly exacted from their subjects. Gongs, socketed or cast missile-heads and other objects, whose origins are north of the Zambezi, make their appearance, suggesting that the Rozwi had some Congo connections.

Plates 33–36

Rozwi sites are widespread throughout Rhodesia, and are readily identified by their fine polychrome band and panel pottery. Class 4 ware at Zimbabwe is almost identical with

some of the later Rozwi pottery from Khami and Dhlo-Dhlo, *Fig. 37*
but polychrome ware is absent except in superficial deposits. The later polychrome pottery industries are more common in Matabeleland than in the east, but Class 4 pottery is present in some of the Ruins in the Fort Victoria region and in the Sabi Reserve and it is thought to extend into Mozambique. Rozwi ruins and pottery are found north of Salisbury and in the Sipolilo region of the Zambezi valley. They are also widespread in the Tati region and throughout Matabeleland as far north as Wankie, only 70 miles from the Victoria Falls.

By the middle of the fifteenth century, the Rozwi *Mambos* were in firm control of the Karanga nation. As well as being in contact with some of their less fortunate neighbours, the Rozwi kings were strongly influenced by Arab traders. These had set up a network of trading stations throughout Karanga country. The political and social influence of the foreign traders was subtle and is easy to underestimate. Abraham has drawn attention to the vital role that Arab policy and strategy played in the events of the following centuries. The Arabs' aim was to furnish themselves with an effective umbrella under which they could expand their commercial operations in an atmosphere of political security. It is likely that it was the Arab traders and their agents who fostered the empire-building desires of their Rozwi clients.

About 1440, according to Abraham, the Rozwi king Mutota launched a major military campaign to secure for his own ends a vast region of Southern Africa, bounded by the Indian Ocean, the Limpopo and Zambezi rivers and the Kalahari Desert. Beyond Arab strategy, there were other impelling reasons for territorial expansion. The Karanga homeland was becoming overpopulated as a result of increasing economic activity, and salt supplies, a vital commodity to any agricultural people, were becoming scarce.

Mutota assembled a large army and by a series of energetic campaigns had subjected most of the present-day Rhodesia, except its eastern borders, by 1450. The Arabs from his homeland followed in his rear, expanding their commercial network as far north as the Zambezi valley. As a result of his victories, Mutota was given the praise name *Mwene Mutapa* (master pillager) by his victims, a name which was perpetuated as Monomotapa, the name of the chiefs of the vast domain now under Mutota's control. His son, Mutope, continued the campaign of conquest over the following thirty years. He finally succeeded in conquering the regions between Karanga-land and the ocean, moving his headquarters and the centre of his vast empire into the northern parts of the domain adjoining the Zambezi valley.

Mutope himself was able to keep his large kingdom together by a system of vassalage. However, tenuous lines of communication, political intrigue and cultural differences inevitably led to the rapid disintegration of the new empire into a number of component parts. The Rozwi vassal, Changa, placed in charge of the southern parts of the Monomotapa's domain by Mutope, immediately began to transform his authority into that of an independent ruler. After Mutope's death in about 1480, he openly flouted the authority of the new Monomotapa, Nyahuma, by changing his name to Changamire. After conquering Nyahuma in battle in about 1490, he ruled the entire empire for four years. Nyahuma's son, Kakuyo Komunyaka, eventually staged a come-back and killed Changamire I, whose own son retained control of only his father's original lands. By a series of diplomatic moves, the latter was able to seduce the eastern and south-eastern parts of Kakuyo Komunyaka's empire from loyalty towards the Monomotapa. Komunyaka was left in effective control of the northern half of Rhodesia and a strip of country about two hundred miles across, running east and south-east to the Indian Ocean. This was the situation with which the Portuguese were confronted at the time of their arrival at Sofala in about 1505.

The logbooks of Vasco da Gama, reporting on his passage up the East Coast from the Cape of Good Hope and across the Indian Ocean in 1488–9, had astonished the Portuguese with their accounts of the wealth and civilization of the African Coast. Further voyages followed and led to a ruthless commercial exploitation of the Coast. Portuguese mariners and warriors wrecked the fabric of the East Coast trade and bent the markets of the Indian Ocean to their own ends.

As part of this campaign, the Portuguese established a small settlement at Sofala. Administratively, the whole of the South East Africa region came under the orders of the Viceroy in Goa on the other side of the Ocean. Much, therefore, depended on the Captain of Mozambique and Sofala. As the Captaincy was usually purchased, the standard of administration was low. From the early sixteenth century, the increasing involvement of the Portuguese with the political events of the Interior has led to a considerable number of historical documents surviving to this day.

The events of the Portuguese period need not concern us in detail. A *degradado*, or pardoned criminal, named Antonio Fernandes was the first Portuguese explorer to enter the country of Monomotapa in about the year 1514. He was sent to discover routes into the interior and to investigate the food supplies available en route. Fernandes' report on his two journeys has survived. There is considerable controversy as to the routes he took. He must have followed the routes of the Arabs or the indigenous traders, visiting the gold-mining districts of Mashonaland, the Mazoe valley and the Lomagundi district. This intrepid traveller may even have visited the Zambezi valley. Zimbabwe was not on his itinerary, but he had discussions with Chikuyu, the Monomotapa of the day, and they parted on amicable terms. As a result of Fernandes' favourable report, the Portuguese made concerted, if slow, efforts to develop trading relations with the Monomotapa. By the middle of the sixteenth century, they had effective commercial and political relations with the interior, and had established outposts at Sena and Tete in the Zambezi valley.

Portuguese policy led to increasing tension between the colonists and the vested interest of the Arabs, who for centuries had kept the monopoly of the Monomotapa's trade and had enjoyed considerable political influence. Matters came to a head when the Arabs succeeded in persuading Monomotapa Nogomo to have Father Silveira, the Roman Catholic priest who had baptized him, put to death. This direct challenge to the Portuguese led to military intervention and an expedition, under Francisco Barreto in 1572, ended in disastrous failure and the death of Barreto himself. A treaty between the two parties was concluded in 1575, under the terms of which the Arabs were to be expelled and mining concessions were to be granted to the Portuguese. During the period 1575–1666, the Portuguese were able to effect steady penetration of Monomotapa's territory and the Arab influence in the north declined. A network of trading stations under the nominal jurisdiction of the Monomotapa was founded, the principal being Masapa, near the Mazoe river, already in existence by 1575. The Monomotapa himself had become dependent on Portuguese power for his position. The Portuguese also penetrated the southern kingdom of Changamire, but less fruitfully.

Plate 32

Relations between the Monomotapa and the Portuguese became increasingly uneasy in the late seventeenth century, and the Changamire of the day, Dombo, was eventually prevailed upon by a usurper to the seat of Monomotapa, known as Nyakambiro, to drive the Portuguese from the interior. Dombo succeeded in doing this in a ruthless military campaign in 1693–1695, which brought him to the very gates of Tete, ravaging and killing the Portuguese population on the way. The Monomotapa and his successors were deprived of most of their country, leaving them with a narrow tract of territory between the Mukumbwa and Rwenya rivers. In due course the Portuguese were obliged to recognize the political ascendancy of Changamire Dombo, and their relations with him and his successors had a direct effect on the efficiency of their trade. Puppet Monomotapas continued to rule a small segment of country within the Portuguese sphere of influence around Sena and Tete. The scope of Portuguese trade depended entirely on the policy of the ruling Changamire, who was strong enough to dominate both them and the Monomotapa on occasion. Caravans under the command of African and half-caste merchants were now despatched from Zumbo or Feira at the confluence of the Luangwa and Zambezi into Changamire's country whenever conditions permitted, but their journeys were hazardous and often ended in disaster. The Portuguese also turned their attention to the north and to the ivory of the Luangwa valley, whence they travelled to Kazembe's country and eventually to Angola. It was not until the 1880's that the Portuguese re-established their political control of the Lower Zambezi, under the stimulus of political competition from other European countries.

The history of political and social events revealed by the documentary record of the Portuguese and the oral traditions of the Karanga says little about the daily lives of the indigenous population and a return must be made to the archaeological record to study the material culture and architecture of the later phases of Rozwi ascendancy.

Excavations have been conducted at a number of Ruin sites which can be dated to the sixteenth–eighteenth centuries, but only at the Khami Ruins near Bulawayo has any detailed work been done. Robinson worked on the Khami sites intermittently from 1947 to the late 1950's, amplifying the limited scientific investigations of early excavators. The principal building is the

Fig. 39

Hill Ruin, which consists of a terraced hill with three distinct terraces. On the top of the citadel are the remains of a number of buildings, probably belonging to a person of some importance. The eastern slopes of the Hill form a cliff, dropping into the river gorge, the topography of the kopje being modified by the three terraces. The latest platform, C, forms the top of the Hill. A passage leads up from platform B below it, to the summit, and ends in a semicircular hut there. Both platforms A and B are on the south side of the Hill, one above the other. Retaining walls are built on the borders of the platforms, parts of one of them being decorated with a chequer pattern. Battering effects are also used, each section of the wall being slightly stepped back. Earth and stones were used for in-filling to the level of the walls, which were heightened several times. At least seven hut sites are to be seen. Between them, traces of stone walling can be discerned, which were originally connected to the houses by pole and daga radial walls. The passage leading up from the B platform appears to have been roofed with daga supported on poles and to have formed a private access route to the summit. Another entrance to the hill-top lies on the north-western side of the hill, consisting of a passage with steps.

Plates 37–40

Plate 38

Plate 37

A second Ruin lies immediately to the north of the Hill Ruin, and consists of a platform, some 80 feet across, raised about 20 feet above ground level and bounded by a well built wall. The remaining buildings are scattered over the ruin field and include several fine examples of walls decorated with

Fig. 39. Plan of Khami Ruins passage complex. a. sites of huts; b. hut Cb1; c. daga steps; d. upper passage way; e. side chamber; f. terrace walling; g. terraced slopes; h. middle passage way; i. boulder; j. lower passage way; k. interconnecting stone and daga walls. Heavy black lines indicate stone walls and black dots posts.

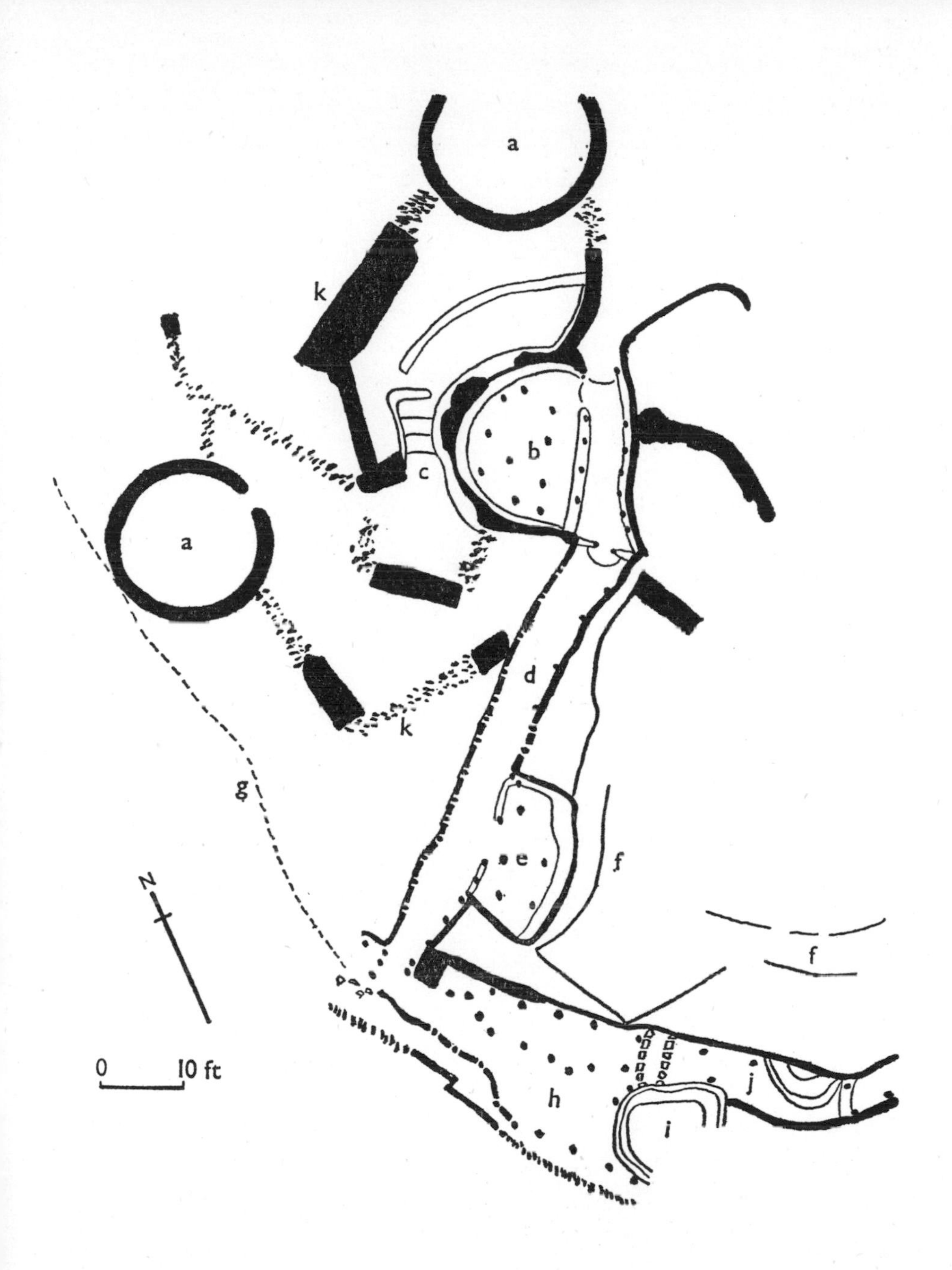
a
k
b
c
a
d
k
g
e
f
N
f
0
10 ft
h
j
i

chequer-pattern work. Middens are also associated with the huts and ruins. The focal point of the Khami sites was obviously the Hill Ruin, the summit of which was occupied by important chiefs or ritual leaders.

All the buildings now visible at Khami are based on the idea of a raised platform supporting huts of daga, wood and thatch. Associated with the platform and sometimes attached to it are livestock enclosures, bounded by free-standing walls.

Architecturally, the Khami buildings are skilfully constructed, but less so than Zimbabwe. Most of the walling is in the form of retaining walls, with some free-standing enclosures. Rectangular or triangular blocks of granite are used for the walling, and the walls are faced with dressed and sized blocks, with a rubble of stone waste for the core of the wall. Blue-coloured dolerite slabs are used as decorative courses and chevron or chequer patterns are found, with occasional zones of herring-bone patterns and some engraved rocks. At Khami, wood and daga were at least as essential to the buildings as stone. Daga was used to give strength to stone structures and for foundations of huts, about 14 to 30 feet in diameter. Walls of daga applied to poles were from 8 to 14 inches thick. Wooden beams were used as supports for roofs, especially in the passageway leading up to the principal hut. Thatch was the usual roofing material.

The focus of the Hill Ruin and, indeed, of all the ruins, was the hut known as Cb1. The general appearance of this building is of a hut cut in half with a sunken floor and thick walls, and it differs strikingly from the usual houses at Khami. The missing half of the house is represented by a raised platform, the retaining wall of which acts as a wall of the hut. Leading into the hut is the passageway from the foot of the hill, which probably gave secret access to the summit. It was clearly roofed over, for the traces of the wooden roof supports can still be seen in the stone walls which line the passage. The filling of

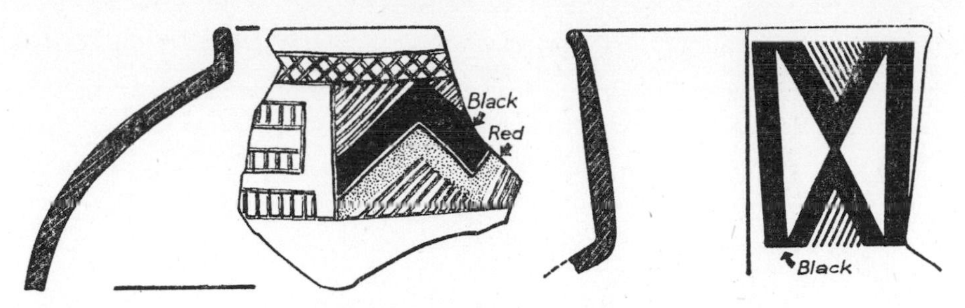

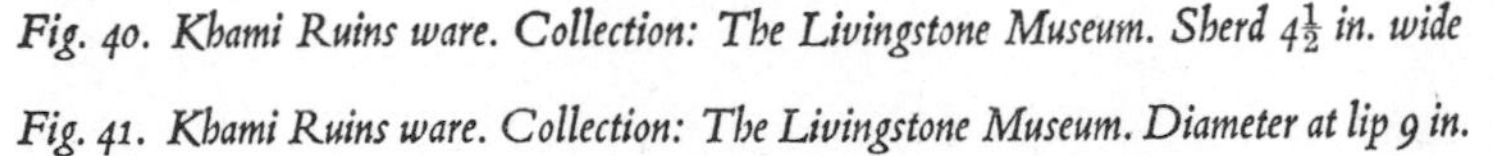
Fig. 40. Khami Ruins ware. Collection: The Livingstone Museum. Sherd $4\frac{1}{2}$ *in. wide*

Fig. 41. Khami Ruins ware. Collection: The Livingstone Museum. Diameter at lip 9 in.

the hut showed that it had been destroyed by fire. Numerous small ivory carvings of ceremonial objects were found in the filling. Immediately behind the west wall are three daga steps. On these was found a cache of ceremonial bronze and iron tools. There is a strong inference from these objects and those in Cb1 itself, that the hut at the end of the passage was some form of relic house or ceremonial hut. It is surprising, though, that the ceremonial objects were abandoned in the hut when it was destroyed. A sudden catastrophe such as a raid might have led to the destruction of the huts of the Rozwi *Mambo* before the sacred relics could be recovered. A pot of possible Swazi manufacture was found in Cb1, together with two axes. These objects may be evidence of a destructive Swazi raid on Khami during the early nineteenth century.

Plate 40

Finds of imported china and stoneware at Khami have been dated to the late sixteenth or early seventeenth century. Robinson considers that these finds were looted from a Portuguese settlement during the time of Rozwi unrest in the 1690's. The beads from the Rozwi occupation can be assigned to the period of Portuguese trade, rather than to Arab sources. Some of the beads are closely related to those from the apparently contemporary site of Dhlo-Dhlo, dated to the seventeenth century. By combining the evidence from imported objects and Rozwi

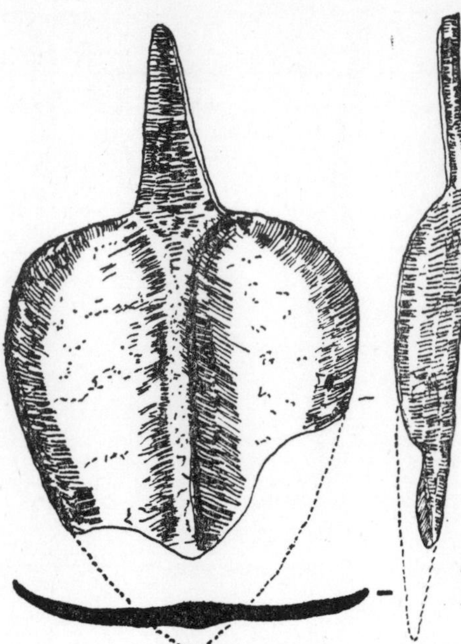

Fig. 42. A hoe from Khami. 9⅜ in. high. After Robinson, 1959

history, Robinson has suggested that Khami was built about 1700 and was occupied for just over a century.

Khami Ruins ware is characterized by the use of polychrome band and panel decoration, especially on spherical and spheroidal pots and occasional beakers. The decoration may be in zigzags, bands or panels. Fluted necks made by drawing the fingers across the clay occur, but undecorated vessels of varying quality are common. Bowls are rare. In general, the standard of manufacture is high and extensive use is made of graphite burnish. Polychrome pottery is also characteristic of other late Rozwi ruins, such as Dhlo-Dhlo.

Figs. 40, 41

Gold objects are uncommon in the Khami deposits. A number of beads was recovered during Robinson's exavations, and it is probable that the *Mambos* of Khami demanded the metal as tribute from their mining neighbours. Copper was made into bangles and alloying was known. Ironworking was not an important activity at the Ruins themselves, but was practised in the region. Some of the iron implements were imported, a socketed spearhead from the hut Cb1 probably being of Congo origin. A study of the material culture from any of the western ruins, or from Zimbabwe for that matter, clearly indicates that the Rozwi culture, as represented in the Ruins, is directly descended from that of the earliest Zimbabwe wall builders during Period III. Foreign influences became absorbed into the original culture as time went on and caused changes in details of the material culture, but the basic nature of the social organization appears to have remained very much the same throughout the centuries.

Fig. 42

The reason for the long survival of this form of culture may be due to the social organization of the Rozwi. Close religious ties between the king as the controller of the *Mwari* cult and the people led to conservatism in customs and material culture. Robinson has also shown that there are ample reasons to prove that there was much in common between the organization of the Monomotapas and that of the Rozwi Mambos.

CHAPTER X

The Inyanga People

THE EASTERN BORDER of Rhodesia lies amongst the Inyanga mountains, which form part of the chain of high peaks bordering the African plateau all the way from the Cape of Good Hope to Ethiopia. Whilst these mountain areas are not particularly fertile or favourable for livestock, they were settled at an early stage in the Iron Age and form an interesting adjunct to the history of the main plateau regions of Mashona-land.

Although the most characteristic monuments in this moun-tain area are the terraces of the later Iron Age, agricultural settlement in the eastern regions goes back many centuries earlier. The Ziwa peoples of the Eastern Districts, whose pottery is related to Gokomere ware, have already been men-tioned. It is known that the earliest Ziwa peoples occupied the Inyanga region in the early first millennium, and that they lived there until at least AD 1050. Stratigraphical evidence from archaeological work at the 'Place of Offerings' ruin and else-where has demonstrated that Ziwa ware pre-dates the Inyanga terraces.

Inyanga was subsequently occupied by peoples who, to judge from the Ruin ware on the Uplands, were of Shona stock, and were responsible for the stonework to be found on the highlands today. The most obvious traces of their activities are cultiva-tion terraces, many of them faced with stone walls. In places the terracing is massive and regular. Most of the walling is rough and uncoursed and walls may be as high as 6 feet on steep slopes. Seen from the air, or when surveyed, the walls give a striking example of contoured terracing. The contour walls may be broken by steep, stone-laid pathways, which take the shortest and steepest way up a slope whilst wider trackways cut

Plates 41-42

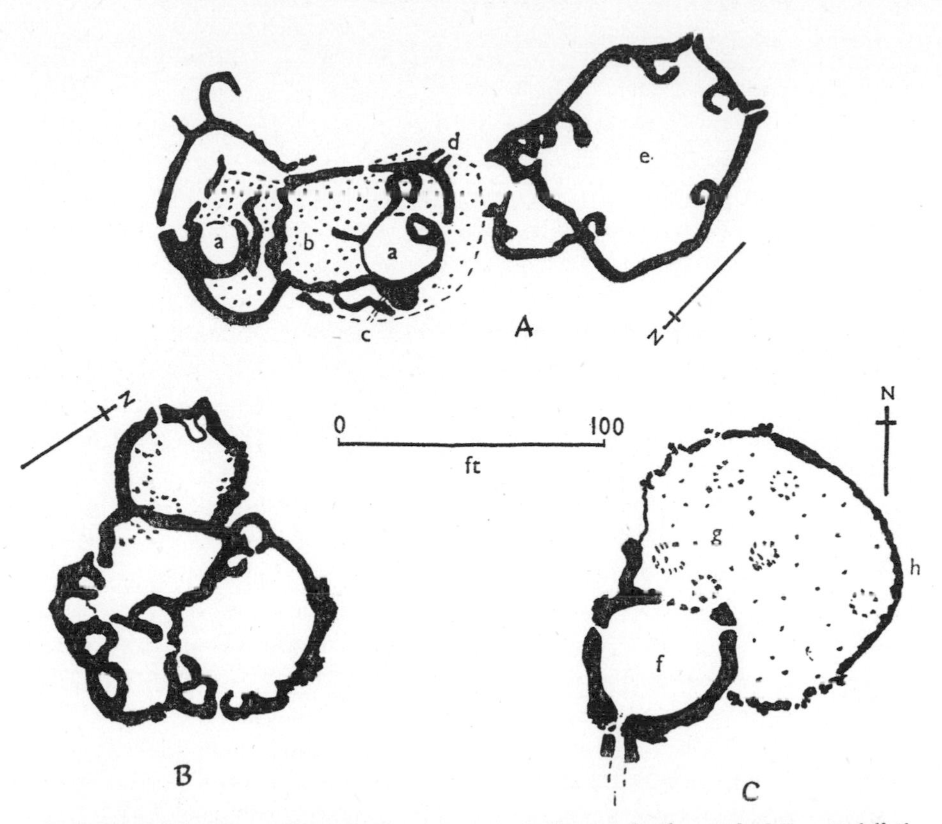

Fig. 43. Plans of three types of Inyanga structures. A, pit dwelling complex from Upland Zone. B, hillside enclosure designed in three units. C, enclosures associated with agricultural terracing. After Whitty, 1959. a, pits; b, artificial earth platform; c, drain from pit; d, entrance of access tunnel to pit; e, large walled enclosure; f, walled enclosure; g, artificial platform of earth; h, retaining wall; i, passage cutting through terrace walling to open ground

the terraces at an angle. Water furrows were built for drainage and irrigation purposes and may extend for several miles from a perennial stream. The most characteristic structures at Inyanga are stone-lined pits, to be found as a general rule above 5,000 feet. These consist of a circular or elliptical pit, about 20 feet in diameter, and 6 to 10 feet deep. Part of the pit is excavated out of the hillside, and the remainder surrounded by a wall built on ground level. The pits are usually paved with stone slabs, giving a gently sloping bottom to the pit. A surround, between 6 and 20 feet wide, consisting of a solid platform, covers two outlets from the pit. One is a drainage hole, the other a curved passage about 4 feet high and 2 feet wide, leading out to the open beyond the boundary of the platform. A carefully built light shaft from the passage appears to have opened into the floor of a daga hut, traces of which were often found on the platform. Occupation middens often occur near by. Local tradition suggests that these pits were used as enclosures for small livestock and perhaps calves. The animals were driven into the pit at night, the passage sealed with sticks passed down through the light shaft, leaving them safe from theft or predators. Pits are confined to the Upland zone at Inyanga. Their counterparts in the lower areas were enclosures of several different types. Some resemble the Upland pits, but are smaller; they are built on sloping ground, the platform being surrounded with a wall pierced by a lintelled doorway and with a passage entrance opposite leading down into the pit.

Fig. 43

Of less frequent occurrence are a number of strongly constructed forts with thick outer walls and often a parapet walk. The walls are pierced with square loopholes, perhaps for imported firearms. These buildings are found throughout the Upland regions of Inyanga and are sited to give shelter and a good view of the country.

It has proved difficult to date Inyanga structures, for radiocarbon dates are not available and one is obliged to rely on imported objects, rare in this remote and economically unimportant region. In the lowlands, Summers and his colleagues examined two major sites, the van Niekerk Ruins and the Nyamombgwe group. A fragment of bottle glass from a hut floor from site XVA on the southern slopes of Ziwa Mountain has been assigned to the eighteenth century, and the associated pottery, of a type found in the van Niekerk Ruins, shows that

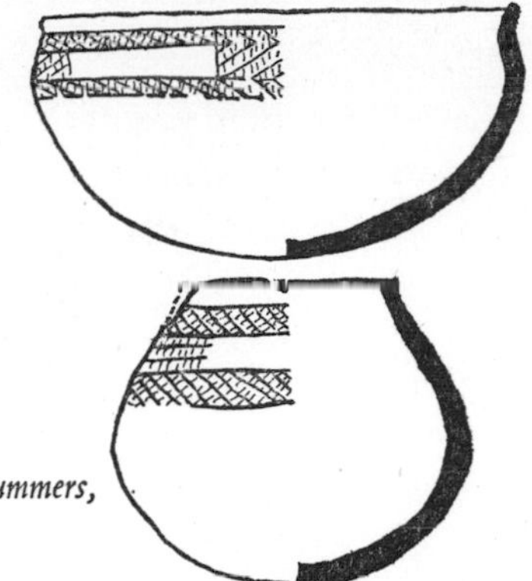

Fig. 44. Inyanga Ruin ware. 1 : 8. After Summers, 1958

the latter belongs to approximately the same period. Direct dating evidence for the Upland ruins was obtained by finds of sixteenth- to eighteenth-century glass and copper beads in a sealed context within a pit platform and under a wall from Nyangwe fort.

There is a gradual evolution in the development of the Inyanga buildings. The sequence begins with the stone-lined pit common on the Uplands, continues with the pit enclosures found at van Niekerk and ends with the small circular enclosures found more commonly in the Nyamombgwe group of ruins. Since the dated Upland sites seem to be slightly earlier than van Niekerk and the settlement pattern at Nyamombgwe differs sufficiently from the latter to suggest a difference in date, it is possible that the sequence of buildings may straddle several different centuries; but there are few variations in the pottery, suggesting that the development of the buildings took place over a short period. The indications are that Inyanga was occupied by terrace cultivators from the sixteenth to eighteenth centuries.

The material culture of the Inyanga people seems impoverished when compared with that of their extravagantly rich neighbours of the Mashonaland plateau. Ruin wares from Inyanga vary considerably amongst themselves and are of a lower standard of finish than the Ziwa pottery which preceded

Fig. 44 them. The pottery from the Upland sites is of poor quality and takes the form of small vessels, mostly deep bowls or shouldered pots. Decorated vessels are unknown. More regular forms occur in the van Niekerk Ruins and consist, for the most part, of shouldered or spheroidal pots. Deep bowls also occur, but shallow vessels are uncommon. The finish is better and bands of incised rectilinear patterns occur on the shoulders of pots.

A type of ware known as 'Ribbed pottery' is found in the Inyanga sites. Spherical or spheroidal pots with short concave necks are decorated with raised clay ribs, forming a lattice pattern around the neck. The ware is usually graphited. Inyanga Ruin ware can be compared with some of the plainer Class 2–4 pottery from Zimbabwe, and somewhat similar ware is distributed over a wide area of Rhodesia. The ribbed pottery of Inyanga is found at Zimbabwe in the Acropolis and Maund Ruins. Ribbed sherds were recovered from a pre-Mosque level at Gedi on the Kenya Coast. Kirkman dates the ribbed vessels there to the twelfth century, and considers them ancestral to the Rhodesian ribbed pottery, which was introduced to the gold-mining regions by coastal people acting as middlemen between Arab traders on the Coast and gold-miners of the Interior. Until more is known of the distribution of Ribbed Ware in Central Africa, Kirkman's speculation must be respected.

Only the simplest of iron objects came from the Ruins. They include spearheads and arrowheads, some with barbs, razors and the keys of hand pianos. Isolated copper or bronze beads and wire fragments were also recovered. The whole feeling of the culture is one of impoverishment and remoteness from the main stream of cultural development.

We know little of the subsistence economics of the other Rhodesian ruins, but the Inyanga economy is better known from Summers' work. Sorghum, bulrush millet, finger millet, maize, bambara groundnuts and various cucurbits were cultivated, using terraced fields. All these crops are grown in almost any part of Rhodesia today and do not require very fertile conditions, and hence were suitable for the Inyanga hill-sides. Wild produce, including the castor oil bean, was collected. Both cattle and small livestock were kept and game was hunted.

As far as we can see, the Inyanga terracing developed independently of influence from other areas where it is found. Terrace cultivation during Iron Age times is recorded from central and north Tanganyika, and the Transvaal, as well as in other parts of Central and North Africa, but there is no reason to connect these with Inyanga, where the technique developed as a result of the geographical features of the agricultural land.

It is striking that there is no occupation of the lowland regions at Inyanga between the end of the Ziwa sequence and the occupation of the van Niekerk Ruins in the eighteenth century. The Uplands over 5,000 feet were settled in the fifteenth and sixteenth centuries, and one wonders why such an unattractive environment was preferred to the more favourable lowland. Undoubtedly, there was some adverse climatic or political condition which led to the abandonment of the lowland. Summers has suggested that the reason for the occupation of the relatively infertile hill country was that the region was settled by immigrants from the north, from the hilly regions of Southern Malawi, where pressure on land by tribesmen from the Congo basin had caused the population to move south. There seem to be similarities in architecture, albeit in different materials, between Inyanga and Chewa peoples from the eastern parts of Zambia. It is clear from comparative studies that there are resemblances between the pottery of the lowland ruins and those of the modern Inyanga tribes, showing a degree of continuity since the Ruin occupation.

Doke has studied the dialects of the Shona of Rhodesia and has shown that the languages of the present Inyanga tribes are related to the Sena group of Bantu languages of the lower

Zambezi, which is a relative of the Nsenga group of languages from Zambia. Antonio Fernandes mentions the Barwe and Wesa in his travels, as if there was a pocket of Nsenga-speakers on the eastern borders of the Shona country by the sixteenth century. Kirkman's ribbed ware from Kilwa also indicates a northern origin for the Inyanga builders, whose pit enclosures are foreign to the builders of the Rhodesian ruins.

It seems probable that the Inyanga complex was built by northern immigrants, linguistically related to the Nsenga group of Zambia. Due to intermarriage and cultural contact, they were considerably influenced by their Shona neighbours of Mashonaland, although the basic features of the Inyanga material culture have survived to this day. The terraces and ruins were probably abandoned as a result of the political pressures from Ngoni raiders in the nineteenth century.

The forts of the Uplands may have been built as a result of the terrible Zimba invasions in the late sixteenth century. The Zimba hordes are only known from Portuguese records, but they are thought to have descended upon the East African Coast and Central Africa from the north, ravaging the country as they went and eating their captives. Zimba raiders were in the Tete region in 1570, and attacked the Portuguese settlements in 1585. They withdrew to Kilwa and the Kenya coast about 1592, but must have penetrated the western parts of Mozambique during their sojourn in the Zambezi valley, giving rise to fear amongst the Inyanga tribes, and the building of fortifications.

Plate 32

CHAPTER XI

Zambia: AD 1200–1800

THE MIDDLE PHASE of the Zambian Iron Age was a period of considerable importance, for it was during that time that Zambia was peopled by the tribes of Congo origin who inhabit the country today. Many early farming groups came under the sway of their more powerful neighbours and have now become part of the tribal structure of their rulers.

Southern Zambia is occupied by Ila/Tonga speaking peoples, whose arrival is thought to have been earlier than the movements of Congo tribes into the country from about 1500 onwards. The Ila and Tonga are cattle-owning people, whose social and political organization is far less complex than that of their northern and western neighbours. Tonga material culture is simple, and their speech contains certain archaic words which are not in general use amongst the other tribes of Zambia. Various speculations have been made about Ila/Tonga origins, and Smith and Dale have recorded a tradition amongst the Ila that they came from the north around Lake Tanganyika many centuries ago. The archaeological evidence from Sebanzi Hill, Lochinvar indicates that the ancestors of the Tonga were living there at least 750 years ago. Wherever the Ila and Tonga may have come from, however, there can be little doubt that they are some of the oldest Bantu peoples to be living in Zambia today.

It must have been during the middle stages of the Zambian Iron Age that the copper mining industries of Katanga and the Zambian Copperbelt were first developed. Copper objects, probably from Zambian mines, occur in a number of first-millennium sites, but the origin of the metal used to make them is unknown. The abundant copper from the Ingombe Ilede in the Zambezi valley may be of Zambian origin, but as a general rule it seems that copper, even for domestic ornament, is rare in first millennium Zambian sites, especially away from the early trade routes. We have still to investigate an early Iron Age site near the copper regions and may find a different picture there. Judging from Jacques Nenquin's excavations at Sanga, near Lake Kisale in Katanga, in which fine copperwork is abundant, the Katanga mines were in production by AD 900 and there is no reason to suppose that the Copperbelt mines were not then functioning. The geographer Pigafetta, writing in 1591, tells of the copper mines of Bembe, which were probably in Angola, Katanga or Zambia. In the closing years of the sixteenth century an Englishman named Andrew Battell spent some time in Angola as a prisoner of the Portuguese. He described peoples trading copper to the coast and centre of Angola from the far interior, perhaps another early reference to the Katanga or Copperbelt mines. One reason for the rarity of copper trade objects in earlier Zambian sites may be the fact that the Katanga copper mines and commercial organizations were attuned to the West Coast and the Angola-Congo markets, rather than the eastern routes which, in the heyday of Monomotapa, seem to have been orientated towards the Rhodesian mines. It was only when Changamire obtained control of central and northern Mashonaland that the Zambezi traders paid more attention to the Luangwa and Kafue routes.

How much copper and gold went south from the Zambian and Katanga mines to the Mashonaland kingdom, we do not know. There has been a tendency to over-estimate the contribution of the Zambian mines to the prosperity of Monomotapa's empire. Nenquin, in his Sanga report, draws attention to the distribution of copper crosses along the Lualaba river and suggests that there was little direct contact between the Katanga markets and those of Zimbabwe. One East Coast cowrie shell came from a Kisalian burial at the Sanga site, but it is an isolated specimen, suggesting that contact with Eastern routes was but sporadic. If this is true of the Kisalian culture in the seventh to ninth centuries, it must have been even more true during the second millennium, when the great Congo kingdoms developed.

When the Portuguese discovered the estuaries of the Congo in 1482, they found themselves in contact with one of the largest states in Sub-Saharan Africa, the kingdom of the Kongo. This 'Sudanic' kingdom had been founded in the late fourteenth or early fifteenth centuries, and may have been an offshoot of the earlier Luba kingdom of Katanga. From the late fifteenth to the late sixteeenth century, the missionary and commercial efforts of the Portuguese were concentrated on this kingdom rather than Angola, but from 1575 they extended their sphere of influence beyond the boundaries of Kongo, in their search for slaves for the Brazilian colonies. Beyond the upper Kwango, between the river and the upper Kasai and eastwards to the Lualaba valley, lived the Lunda. Their traditional history extends back to the sixteenth century, before which they seem not to have had any state organization or powerful chieftainship. During the late 1500's, a small group of Luba ivory hunters appeared amongst them, and proceeded to build up a feudal state, headed by a dynasty of chiefs named Mwata Yamvo. From the very start of its existence, Mwata Yamvo's kingdom was in indirect contact with the Portuguese traders of Angola, receiving firearms, ammunition and European luxuries in exchange for ivory. The immediate perimeter of the Portuguese colony was dominated by the slave trade, but outside this frontier ivory was the primary export. In order to maintain steady supplies of ivory, a large-scale political and economic organization is required to control the hunting and handling of the ivory. As Roland Oliver has pointed out, this political and economic expertise already existed in the Luba regions of northern Katanga. By virtue of the centralized organization of the dynasty, a number of peripheral states, subject in name to Mwata Yamvo, sprang up and there was a gradual dispersal of Lunda chieftaincies and their followings to the south-east of the kingdom of Mwata Yamvo and across the Luapula river into Zambia.

It is likely, however, that these were merely part of a whole series of migrations from the Congo into east central Africa during the second millennium. The earliest migrants whose identity has come down to us were the Maravi. Early travellers gave this name several centuries ago to the agglomeration of tribes living north of the Zambezi and on both sides of Lake Nyasa, and it has survived as Malawi to the present day. Today, these peoples form a large ethnic group of Nyanja-speakers, comprising a number of tribes in the Eastern Province of Zambia, central Malawi and the Tete region. Oral traditions regarding the origin of the Maravi differ, but there is general agreement that at least the chiefly dynasty amongst them was of Luba origin, having entered the Nyanja area from the Southern Congo basin by a route which led them past Lake Nyasa. The date of the Maravi migration is not accurately established. Gaspar Bocarro, a Portuguese explorer, crossed overland from Tete to Kilwa on the East Coast in 1616; his account of the journey contains a doubtful reference to Maravi peoples. Manoel Barretto, a Jesuit priest, who lived for a long period in the Lower Zambezi valley, has left us an account of the Maravi, written in 1667. They were warlike people who traded ivory, iron, slaves and coarse cloth with the Portuguese, who, in their turn, passed the trade materials to the Karanga. The date of the Maravi migration may lie as early as AD 1500, a widely accepted date, but they were certainly in the Nyanja region by the seventeenth century.

In the heyday of the Luba-Lunda kingdom of the Mwata Yamvo in the seventeenth and eighteenth centuries, this vast empire stretched across Katanga, and there were further extensive population movements to the south and east from the

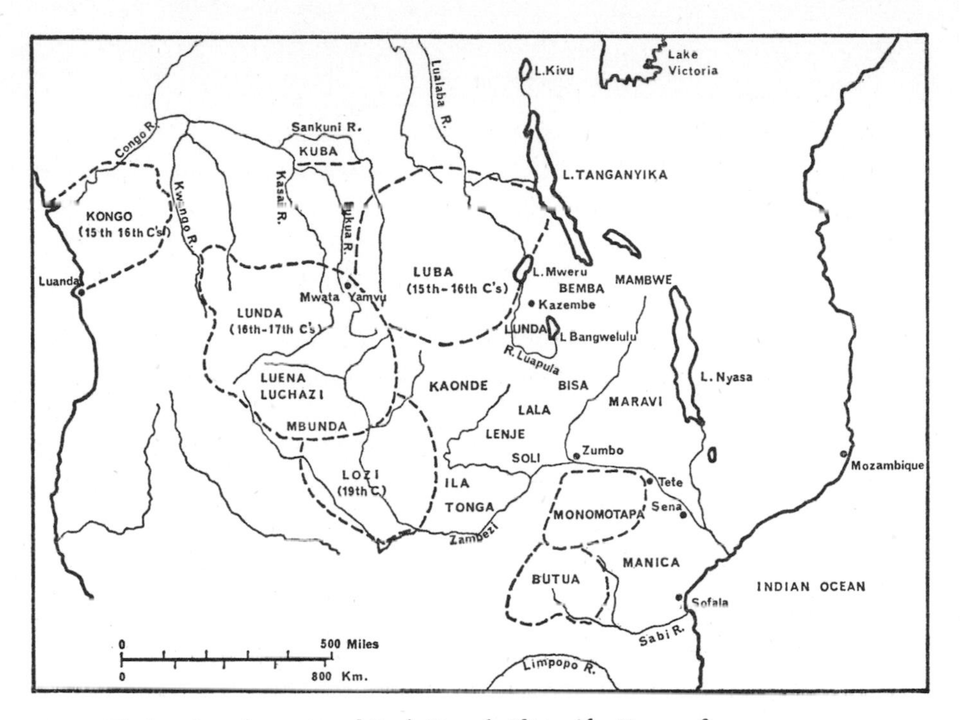

Fig. 45. The later Iron Age empires of South Central Africa. After Fage, 1958

Lunda homeland. According to traditional accounts, Mwata Yamvo I had some half a dozen sons, one of whom succeeded him, whilst the others carved out kingdoms for themselves on the Luapula, the Zambezi-Congo watershed, and in present north-western Zambia. It was during the eighteenth century that the greatest population movements took place across the Luapula.

The Bemba, who today occupy much of the Northern Province of Zambia, are thought to have been the first to cross, in the early eighteenth century. Their exact relationship to the Lunda hierarchy of the time has not been established, but it is known that the Bemba broke away from the main dynasty and spread eastwards under the leadership of one Chiti. They found a number of other Congo tribes there before them, including the Lala, Lungu and Mambwe. After widespread wanderings, the Bemba settled in the Kasama area under the leadership of a line of paramount chiefs known as Chitimukulu. The tribe raided and made forays over a wide area, driving their own kinsmen, the Bisa, to the fringes of the Bangweulu swamps, and demanding tribute from them and other subject groups. Eventually, Chitimukulu held sway over a vast region of much of the Northern and Eastern Provinces. As Bemba rule is characterized by a strongly centralized chieftainship, and a complex hierarchy and political system, there was some stability over the Bemba empire and their culture spread over a large region.

The Bemba were followed by the Lunda, who are thought to have crossed the Luapula about 1740. A group of Lunda, under the predecessor of chief Kazembe was sent eastwards by Mwata Yamvo to gain control of salt deposits in eastern Katanga. The Lunda crossed the Luapula under the leadership of Kazembe some time later. Comparatively small numbers of them were able to dominate the indigenous peoples with the aid of the firearms they had obtained from the slave and ivory trade with Angola. Kazembe settled near Kawambwa, where his dynastic descendant still lives today, and his people settled throughout the Luapula valley, living in amicable relationship with their Bemba cousins to the east. Their copper and iron markets were in the west for, as we have seen, they were based on the provision of ivory, and slaves to carry it, for the Portuguese of Luanda. In contrast to the Bemba tradition of rampage, the Lunda extended their possessions by assimilating other people into their culture and royal dynasty.

Plate 43

North-western and central Zambia is now occupied by a large number of tribes of ultimately Luba origin, including the Lala, Lovale, Southern Lunda, Kaonde, Lamba and Soli. The dates of their respective arrivals are unknown, but prob-

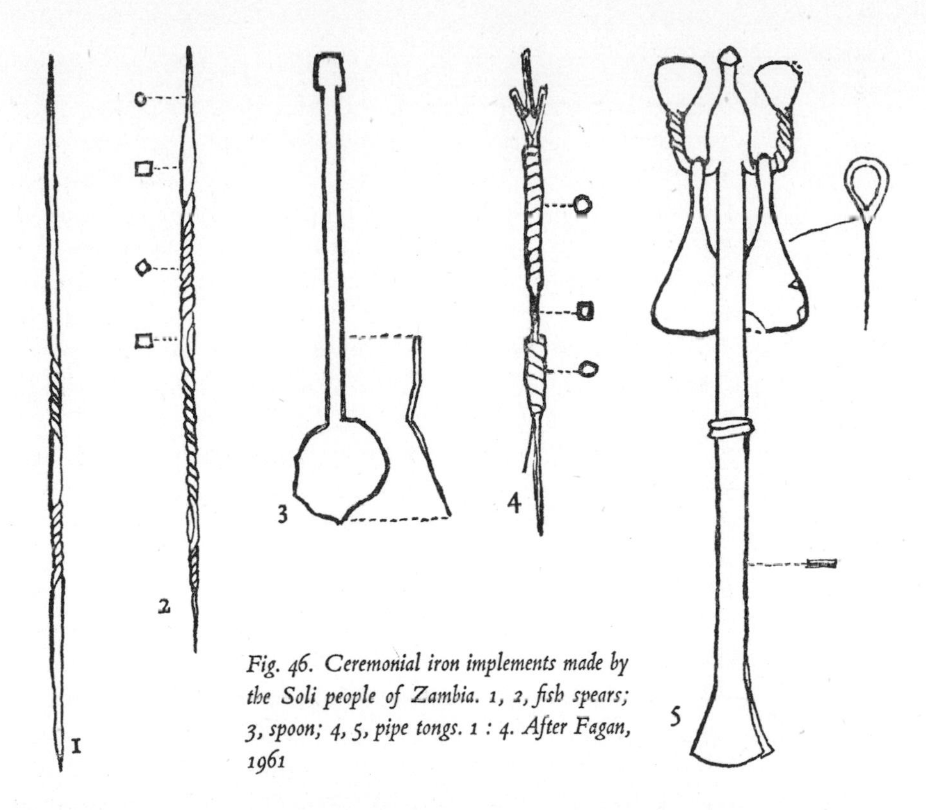

Fig. 46. Ceremonial iron implements made by the Soli people of Zambia. 1, 2, fish spears; 3, spoon; 4, 5, pipe tongs. 1 : 4. After Fagan, 1961

ably lie between the seventeenth and nineteenth centuries. Since most of Zambia was settled by tribes of ultimately Luba origin from perhaps the sixteenth century onwards, it is logical to expect that the material culture and economy over the regions concerned would be standardized. The standardization appears in the metalwork, which reached a high level. Bowstands, staffs and ceremonial iron stools formed part of the chiefly regalia of the Lunda, Bemba, Kaonde, Soli and others. Ceremonial gongs, battle axes, tongs and fine spearheads were made by the blacksmiths, who used a tall iron furnace fired by natural draught. The making of midribs, flange welding and other advanced techniques serve to connect the ironwork with Congo smiths.

Fig. 46

Plates 44, 45

Plates 47, 48

The sand plains of western Zambia and the Zambezi flood-plain are occupied by the Lozi and their dependent tribes. Considerable controversy has raged about the origin of the Lozi chieftainship. Their system of government is strongly centralized on the 'Sudanic' principle, and it is likely that they settled on the Barotse plain and dominated the indigenous inhabitants in the same manner as the Lunda did the Luapula peoples. Both a Lunda/Luba and a Rozwi origin are claimed for the Lozi, but the general consensus of opinion is in favour of the Lunda/Luba theory. Oral tradition indicates that the Lozi kingdom was founded by a female leader named Mwambwa, who moved into Barotseland from the country of Mwata Yamvo in the seventeenth or eighteenth centuries, but there may have been Rozwi influences on the Lozi kingdom. The Lozi empire was subjected to a series of invasions from the south by small numbers of Bechuana in the late eighteenth century and by Kololo in the early 1830's.

Plate 46

We can say that the basic tribal distribution of the present day was established by the beginning of the nineteenth century, but it was affected by political events from the outside, both of Portuguese and African origin. Penetration of the Zambian interior by the Portuguese seems to have started in the eighteenth century. In 1691, Changamire's ravages curtailed commercial exploitation of the Rhodesian markets, and Portuguese merchants turned their eyes to the north. We know from Barretto that the Portuguese were trading with the Maravi of the Zambezi valley in the seventeenth century. The preoccupation of Portuguese policy on the Zambezi during the eighteenth century was firstly with trade in the Zambezi and the Luangwa valleys, emphasized by the foundation of the settlement at Feira at the confluence of that river with the Zambezi in 1721. Secondly, they were anxious to open up a transcontinental route to Angola, thus avoiding the long sea route round the Cape of Good Hope. Feira and its neighbour Zumbo flourished during the eighteenth century. Itinerant Bisa traders, in contact with Kazembe and Mwata Yamvo, visited the Portuguese settlements on the Zambezi.

The Lunda of Katanga had been in indirect contact with the Portuguese on the west coast for some time, through middlemen of the Bangala tribe of the Angolan interior, and had probably heard of the existence of the Portuguese on the East Coast. In 1793, some Bisa tribesmen, trading with the Yao of Malawi, visited a trader living north of Tete and informed him that Kazembe wished to trade with him. The trader sent his son, Manoel Gaetana Pereira, and some African traders to visit Kazembe, who received them favourably with promises of trade in the future. In 1798, Francisco José de Lacerda e Almeida became Governor of the Sena Rivers, with specific responsibility for promoting an expedition to cross to Angola, for the Portuguese, worried by the British occupation of the Cape in 1795, were anxious to open an overland route to the West Coast. An expedition under Lacerda's leadership, was soon mounted, with the object of visiting Kazembe and establishing friendly relations with him, as well as exploring the river system of Central Africa. The Governor unfortunately died at, or near, Kazembe's capital on 18th October, 1798, but the members of the party were well received and stayed at the Lunda capital for seven months. Kazembe refused to grant them permission to go through to Angola and the expedition finally returned to Tete in 1799, without achieving any concrete results, either in terms of exploration or trade.

The possibilities for trade revealed by Lacerda's expedition led the Angolan authorities to send two half-castes, P. J. Baptista and Amaro José, known as the Pombeiros, to attempt the crossing. They arrived at the reigning Kazembe's court on 30th October, 1806, and were detained there until 1810, arriving in Tete during February 1811, and subsequently returning by the same route. The Pombeiros found Kazembe living in some state with a wide range of European goods. His exports were 'ivory, slaves, green stones and copper bars, which they sell to the travellers from Tete and Senna, and to the blacks of the Huiza (Bisa) nation, who are established on the road to Tete'. In spite of the Pombeiros' journey, the promise of better trade was never fulfilled. The final attempt to open up trade with the Lunda came with Monteiro and Gamitto's expedition in 1831–2, which had as sole object the initiating of trading relations with Kazembe. Their attempts were rebuffed and the party returned to Tete after great hardships, without achieving anything. The leaders of the expedition drew up a memorandum in which they stated that the reasons for not continuing trading were overwhelming. Kazembe had recognized the dangers of allowing his powerful commercial neighbours to dominate his key position in the centre of the continent. His position of strength was broken shortly after the Monteiro expedition by the arrival of Arab traders and the ascendancy of the Yeke empire of south-eastern Katanga. The Arabs, in contrast to the Portuguese, were experienced in the political and social climate of Central Africa. Their more subtle methods were able to break the power of the mighty Lunda empire, which had dominated the events of the later Zambian Iron Age for so long.

The pattern of the closing centuries of the Iron Age is of a gradual dispersal of chieftainships of Lunda origin into the northern, eastern and north-western parts of Zambia. In the south-east, earlier Iron Age groups continued to live undisturbed by the important population movements of the Congo basin. With the arrival of Luba peoples, the standards of iron technology and agriculture improved. The population increased and mounting pressure on land made warfare more frequent. Events in the nineteenth century led to profound changes in the political and economic pattern of the Zambian tribes, and we shall return to these in our final chapter.

CHAPTER XII

South Africa: AD 1000–1800

IN AN EARLIER CHAPTER (IV), we showed that Iron Age peoples making Gokomere pottery were settled in the region of the Zoutpansberg mountains by the ninth century AD, if not earlier. We do not yet know how far south these people settled, for the Matokoma site is still an isolated discovery. A radiocarbon date for a furnace at Melville Koppies shows that ironworkers were smelting on the hills of the Witwatersrand by the eleventh century, at which time Smithfield (Later Stone Age) hunters were still living in the Magabengberg and at Olieboompoort.

Fig. 47

The Iron Age peoples of the areas to the north of the Zoutpansberg and of the Middle Limpopo valley were to a certain extent isolated from their neighbours to the south of the mountains, and owed their inspiration to events in the north. For this reason, the later archaeology of the northern parts of South Africa is better known than that of the rest of the Transvaal and other South African provinces.

Revil Mason has recognized two distinct, but probably contemporary, later Iron Age cultures in the Central and Southern Transvaal.

THE UITKOMST CULTURE

The first of the two cultures is known from excavations at five cave sites and an iron-smelting site and from surveys of open-air settlements. Uitkomst sites extend as far north as Warmbaths, but the main focus of the culture lies between the Magaliesberg and the Witwatersrand.

Fig. 16

The earliest dated Uitkomst site is a smelting furnace found at Melville Koppies on the Witwatersrand. Mason, who investigated the find, discovered several iron-smelting furnaces, one at a depth of 12 inches, the others lying close to the surface. The lowermost furnace was a small circular structure, which has been dated to 1060 ± 50 BC by the C14 method, but the smelters on the surface are thought to be more modern. Potsherds found in the vicinity of the lower furnace show that it was used by Uitkomst culture people. Similar pottery came from the ruins of a stone-walled structure on the lower slopes of the hill. The Melville Koppies smelter is evidence that the Uitkomst people had reached the central Transvaal by AD 1000.

At Uitkomst cave, the type site of the culture, 40 inches of Iron Age occupation overlay a Later Stone Age, Smithfield level. Two small iron-smelting furnaces with dome-like chambers and a circular shape with one or more draught holes were found in the deposits, stratified one on top of the other. Radiocarbon tests gave a date of AD 1650 ± 80 for the upper furnace, showing that the Uitkomst occupation dates to the middle phases of the culture. Mason considers that the Uitkomst culture survived until the coming of Europeans in the early nineteenth century, for there are records of stone-built enclosures in the Marico and Rustenburg regions in the neighbouring Buispoort culture area by travellers such as Campbell and Moffat, who visited the region immediately before and after the disastrous Nguni invasions of the 1820's. Robert Moffat gives a succinct description of the sites: 'The ruined towns exhibited signs of immense labour and perseverance, every fence being composed of stones, averaging 5 or 6 feet high, raised apparently without either mortar, lime, or hammer. Everything is circular, from the inner fences which surround each house to the walls which sometimes encompass the town. The remains of some of the houses which escaped the flames of the marauders were large and showed a . . . superior style. . . . The walls were generally composed of clay with a small mixture of cow-dung. . . . The walls and doors were neatly ornamented with archi-

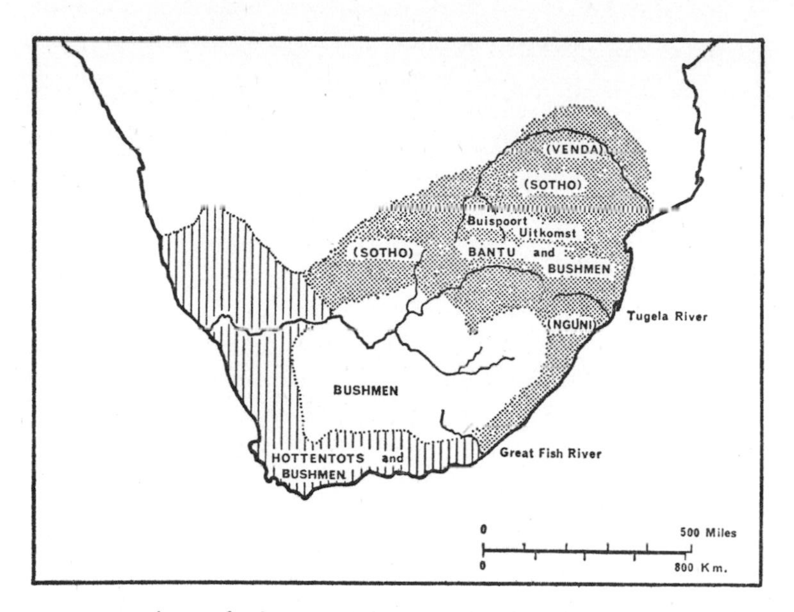

Fig. 47. Distribution of indigenous peoples in South Africa about AD 1652. After Willcox, 1963

traves and cornices, etc. . . . Some of these towns which were at a distance from the materials of which they were composed must have cost much time and labour, as the neighbouring hills gave ample demonstration.'

The Uitkomst people can be regarded as the Transvaal equivalent of Leopard's Kopje culture folk of Rhodesia. Their sites post-date the Gokomere occupation of the Zoutpansberg, and the earliest stages of the culture are contemporary with the Leopard's Kopje site at Greefswald in the middle Limpopo.

Uitkomst culture pottery, described both from the type site and from Tafelkop, consists of deep bowls and the ubiquitous shouldered pot, some of the sherds showing traces of graphite or haematite burnishing. Rim forms are simple, and stamped or incised decoration is predominant. Parallel incised or stamped lines, either continuous or discontinuous, are found and variants on this basic theme are common. It is not yet possible to relate this ware to more northerly Iron Age pottery industries, although there are thought to be some typological connections between Leopard's Kopje and Uitkomst wares.

Of particular interest at Uitkomst are the organic remains. Traces of plaited ropes, strings and mattings are found, and a wooden bowl came from surface levels. The Uitkomst people were also builders in stone and many stone enclosures for cattle are known from their culture area. The best known site is that at Klipriviersberg, where the outer walls surround groups of inner enclosures, the walls being between 3 and 8 feet high. No mortar was used and rubble-filled walls were sometimes constructed. It would be premature to say that there is any connection between the wall builders of this region and their Rhodesian neighbours.

Plate 49

THE BUISPOORT CULTURE

The sites of this culture are to be found in the Rustenburg region of the Transvaal. Stone-walled settlements are characteristic and are very similar to Uitkomst examples. Those at Olifantspoort, investigated by Mason, appear to be better than those at Klipriviersberg. Van Hoeper and Hoffman have also examined Buispoort sites. From the historical descriptions of nineteenth-century travellers such as Campbell, we know that stone walls enclosed whole villages. At Olifantspoort, Mason found that the walls were neatly rounded at the ends and that there were traces of numerous iron-smelting furnaces within the enclosures. The pottery from these western sites is of the same general type as Uitkomst ware, but the decoration is simpler and confined to short vertical strokes or gashes on the rims of the vessels. Iron implements include hoes, spear blades, adzes, and axes but apparently few arrowheads.

Plate 50

The chronology of the Buispoort culture is still unknown, but it is likely that the Uitkomst and the Buispoort people are broadly contemporary.

Mason has drawn attention to the resemblances between Uitkomst and related wares and the pottery of the Sotho-speaking peoples who live in the region today. Furthermore, it is known from historical records that Buispoort stone structures were occupied by Hurutse peoples in the early nineteenth century. There is reason to believe that there was some interaction between both the Uitkomst and Buispoort cultures of the archaeological record and the ancestors of the modern Sotho peoples who are skilled builders in stone to this day.

Settlements similar to those of the Southern Transvaal are known from the grass-land regions of the Lydenburg district, over to the fringes of the Kalahari desert in the west. The enclosures are associated with agricultural terracing, especially near Lydenburg.

There was considerable mining activity during the Iron Age in the central and southern Transvaal. Gold, copper and tin deposits were mined, the latter near Rooiberg. Imported objects are not common in Iron Age sites, indicating that much of the mining was sporadic and designed to satisfy local needs, at any rate in the earlier Iron Age. Some tin may have been traded to the East Coast and Delagoa Bay and it is known that in 1724–5 a Dutch expedition, under Jan van de Capelle, established a fort at Delagoa Bay and traded tin from the Transvaal interior for beads, perhaps supplanting an earlier Arab trade.

THE ORANGE FREE STATE

Some settlements in the northern Orange Free State resemble the southern Transvaal villages. This region is largely treeless today, although it may have been wooded in the past. As a result, corbelled domes of undressed stone were used to replace the thatched roofs of the usual Iron Age hut. Little archaeological work has been carried out in this area, but the pottery is similar in many respects to that from Buispoort. Finger-nail and other impressed techniques were used, as well as the grooved decoration found on the rims of many vessels, as at Buispoort. Some sherds with moulded decoration, of a type which is not found in the Buispoort sites, occur. Although, like the Transvaal settlements, it is probable that many of these villages were destroyed by nineteenth-century warfare, it is impossible to date them with any accuracy. Many of them are probably several centuries earlier and may be the work of early Sotho peoples such as the Fokeng.

NATAL

The Iron Age cultures of Natal are known almost entirely from the coastal regions, where sea-shell middens have yielded potsherds and traces of Iron Age occupation. Schofield, who has studied the pottery of the Coast, was unable to obtain much stratigraphical data from the middens, but he was able to divide the pottery of the region into three distinct groups on a typological basis. One or two fragments of Hottentot pottery, noticeably from Umhloti and Umgababa, comprise the first group. Schofield's middle phase of pottery, his NC_2, is much more common and the sites are more widely spread in the coastal belt and elsewhere in Natal. Globular pots and various types of bowls are especially characteristic of this ware, and they are decorated with notched rim edges, point-mark designs and with closely set finger-nail or incised decorations, with moulded motifs. Pipe bowls are also common. The pottery can be compared to Uitkomst and Buispoort wares. Stone structures are found east of the Drakensberg where wood supplies are abundant, and related vessels may also be discovered in these sites in the future. Since there are resemblances

Fig. 48

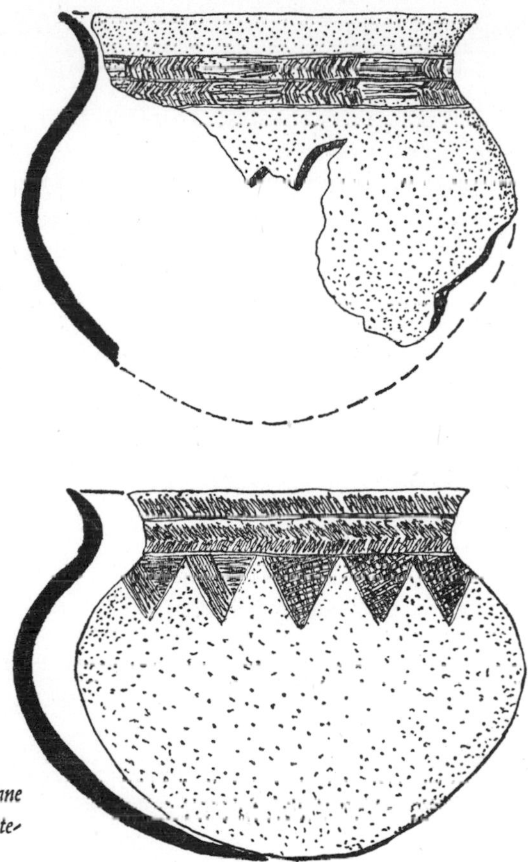

Fig. 48. Natal coastal pottery from Ingane River mouth, Natal. 1 : 6. After Schoute-Vanneck and Walsh, 1959

between Uitkomst and NC_2 pottery, it is probable that there was interaction between the makers of the Natal wares and the ancestors of the same linguistic group.

Much of Natal, then, was probably settled by Sotho peoples from the west or north-west, but we do not know at what date the migrations took place.

In June 1552, the Portuguese galleon 'Sao Joao' was wrecked on the coast of Pondoland, a little way north of the Mzimvubi river. The survivors met parties of cattle herders, but reported that the coast was void of settlements. Two years later, the survivors of the 'Sao Bento' came across 'seven or eight Kaffirs, . . . very black in colour, with woolly hair and went naked'. From this and other descriptions by the same party, there can be little doubt that these were Bantu peoples, who valued metal highly. Forty years later, in March 1593, another vessel, the 'Sant Alberto', was wrecked south of the Mtata river. From the records of the survivors, we know that the inhabitants were Nguni-speakers, and it is at this date that we have our first connection with the modern tribal distribution of South Africa. These Nguni-speakers were dressed in mantles of ox-hide and wore sandals. They cultivated millet and maintained large herds of cattle, which were penned within their villages of low round huts.

The archaeological evidence from northern Natal shows that the people there were more prolific ironworkers. The survivors of the 'Sant Alberto' who, south of the Tugela, had found iron in short supply, discovered that the relative value of their goods changed in the north. Metals were more common and cloth was a more important trade commodity. In northern Natal examples of Schofield's NC_3 pottery are found. This pottery is characterized by concave-necked pots with globular bodies and spherical pots with bands of diagonal cross-hatching, herring-bone or parallel lines at the base of the neck. Schofield has drawn attention to the resemblances between this ware and some isolated vessels from the Limpopo valley sites and Mashonaland, but further work is needed before his observations can be confirmed.

THE ANTHROPOLOGICAL EVIDENCE

As far as can be discovered from historical records of the Natal coast, the present distribution of the Bantu tribes of South Africa has been established for at least 350 years. There must be some degree of contact between the ethnographic and archaeological records, which must be examined in the light of anthropology.

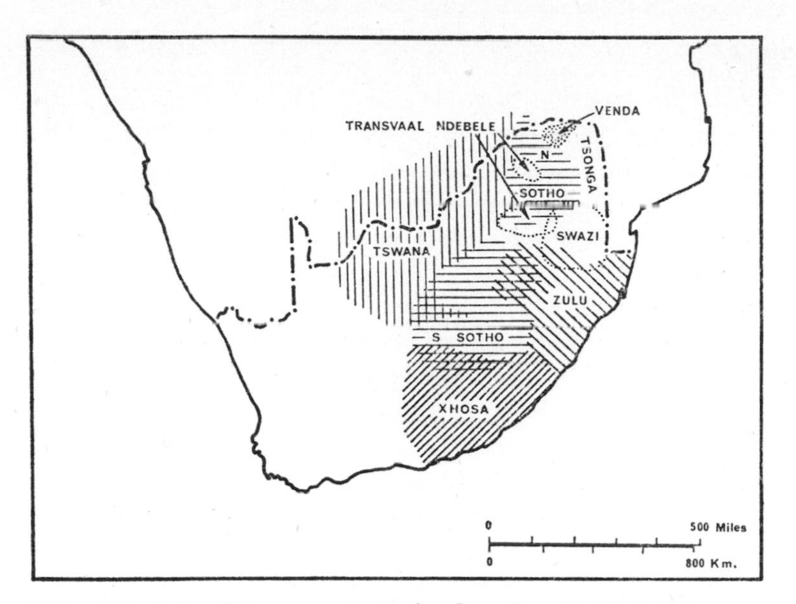

Fig. 49. Distribution of Bantu groups in South Africa today. After Cole, 1961

Van Warmelo has divided the Bantu-speaking tribes of South Africa into four major groups, all of which have been in South Africa for several centuries. The principal subdivisions by language are the Sotho, Nguni, Venda, Lemba, and, lastly, Shangaan-Tonga; the last-named need not concern us here. This grouping is fundamental in the ethnic history of the people, for it is reflected not only in their language and territorial distribution, but also in their cattle and pottery traditions. Since the latter are the most important tools of the archaeologist, it is necessary to concentrate on this trait, which is common to all Iron Age tribes.

Fig. 49

SOTHO

The Sotho extend from northern Bechuanaland southwards into the Transvaal, the Orange Free State and Basutoland. They differ from their Nguni neighbours in details of their social organization and language. The early history of the Sotho tribes is open to conjecture, but it is generally accepted that they came from the north in the first place. The route they followed, the chronology and the ultimate ancestry of the numerous Sotho groups are unknown from oral or written sources. There are three distinct sub-groups of Sotho. The Southern Sotho live in or around Basutoland and, prior to the nineteenth century, were divided into numerous small communities, some of which had entered Basutoland from the west and others from the east. Western Sotho peoples include the Tswana and a number of tribes in the western Transvaal. Little is known about the early history of these groups, but the Tswana are thought to have come southwards along the edge of the Kalahari desert many centuries ago. The Hurutse of the Western Transvaal take precedence amongst many of the Western Sotho peoples, suggesting that they are one of the older and more senior groups. The Eastern Sotho, who live in northern and eastern Transvaal, are represented by the Pedi and other less important tribes; their early history is unknown, but the most powerful people before the Nguni expansion were the Maroteng, who appear to have dominated all the other tribes of the area.

Sotho pottery is divided into three groups, corresponding to the three subdivisions of the Sotho themselves. The groups are distinct, but their typology is obviously linked. Southern Sotho, or Basuto ware is found in a wide diversity of forms and with many decorative motifs. U-shaped brewing pots, finely made cups, and biconical cups are all common. These are treated with a wide range of coloured surface finishes and decorated with incised or comb or bangle impressions, to form a band or line of chevrons on the vessel. Notched rims, like those on Buispoort ware, appear frequently.

The pottery of the Eastern Sotho is very similar to that of the Basuto. Spherical, lenticular or carinated vessels are found, often with short necks. Bands of elaborate incised and impressed decoration in the form of chevrons are common. The Pedi and other Eastern Sotho groups make vessels which are undoubtedly descended from an ancestral ware from Bechuanaland, through intermediate ancient Hurutse and Tswana pottery. Shouldered brewing pots and tumbler-shaped drinking vessels are typical, decorated with a notched comb from a gourd. 'Arcade' decoration is characteristic and probably has its prototype in the pottery of the Uitkomst people.

Sotho pottery undoubtedly belongs to a long-established pottery tradition. There are typological links between Uitkomst and Buispoort wares and the vessels of the Eastern and Western Sotho, which suggest that there was some interaction between the makers of these types of pottery and the ancestors of modern Sotho peoples. Furthermore, the tumbler-shaped vessels of the Pedi, which are found in Buispoort sites, have ancient parallels in Bechuanaland and Limpopo and Leopard's Kopje pottery. Schofield has drawn attention to some 'Sotho' features in the pottery from K2, which can be connected with the Leopard's Kopje culture as well. If these resemblances in the archaeological record are anything to go by, the Sotho population of most of the Transvaal, Orange Free State and Basutoland, is of considerable antiquity, perhaps dating back to the first centuries of the second millennium, if not earlier.

NGONI

The Ngoni tribes live below the central plateau between the Drakensberg and the Indian Ocean and stretch from Swaziland in the north through Natal far into the Cape Province. They are cattle-owning people, with 'click' features in their language, which are thought to have been acquired by contact with Hottentot pastoralists. The Ngoni were the first Bantu peoples to be encountered by the Dutch settlers near the Great

Fish River in 1702. Ngoni peoples have been subdivided into the Mpondo, Swazi, Thembu, Xhosa, Zulu and many other groups. Of these, undoubtedly the strongest were the Zulu, whose empire-building activities have led to the imposition of their culture over much of the Ngoni territory. The political supremacy of the Zulu peoples has resulted in most Ngoni pottery found north of the Mtamvuma being classified as Zulu. Spherical beer pots were decorated with pellets of clay in rectangles, lines or crescents, or with wales of clay raised above the general level of the surface. Stitch-like incision was also used. Similar motifs are found on necked carrying-pots or barrel-shaped drinking vessels. The motifs on the pottery are derived from those carved on the wooden vessels characteristic of Zulu culture.

Little is known of Xhosa or Thembu pottery, but the latter includes notched rims, characteristic of Schofield's NC_2 ware. Mpondo pottery is very similar to Zulu wares, but is coarser. Their spherical pots resemble NC_2 pottery.

The earlier history of the Ngoni is unknown from oral histories, although both Bryant and Soga have attempted to reconstruct their early movements, the former suggesting that the Ngoni crossed the Limpopo about 1400. Captain Gardner suggested, on inadequately published grounds, that the first Bantu peoples to live at K2 were Ngoni. Neither Bryant's chronology nor Gardner's conclusions have stood the test of time, for the evidence is quite inadequate to justify the conclusions drawn. As far as has been established, there is no unequivocal trace of the Ngoni in the archaeological record of Rhodesia or the Limpopo valley. This, since the Ngoni were, for most of their history, essentially nomadic cattle people, is hardly surprising, for wooden vessels and the byproducts of pastoralism rarely survive in the archaeological record. They have, however, been living in their present area for many centuries.

VENDA AND LEMBA

The Venda and Lemba live in the Middle Limpopo valley and in the Zoutpansberg mountains of the northern Transvaal. The latter are also found in Rhodesia. To a certain extent, they have been isolated from the Southern Bantu by their geographical situation, except to the south and south-west. The Venda are characterized by a language akin to Sotho and Karanga and have a distinctive culture, which serves to link them with Rhodesian groups. The royal families of the Venda keep themselves aloof from the commoner, and the relationships between Venda tribes depend on the attitudes of the royal families. Venda pottery is characteristically polychrome and can be linked with the Rozwi wares of Rhodesia. It is generally agreed that the Venda are an offshoot of the Rozwi, with whom they share many ritual practices. Venda peoples are thought to have crossed the Limpopo in the fifteenth or sixteenth centuries, shortly after the Rozwi occupation of Zimbabwe. The new chiefs did not occupy the Shona stronghold at Mapungubwe, but settled elsewhere in the Limpopo valley.

Lemba people were skilful metalworkers and potters, who spoke a dialect of Karanga and lived amongst the Venda by bartering their manufactures in exchange for food. Today, many Lemba and Venda communities are almost indistinguishable. Lemba acted as the metalworkers, traders, and businessmen amongst the Venda and other tribes. Their customs differed in many important respects from those of their Venda associates. No Lemba would eat the meat of an animal whose throat had not been cut before death, and pork was abhorrent to them. They practised circumcision, and are thought to have introduced the rite to the Venda.

Almost nothing is known of the early history of the Lemba, but their distinctive non-Negro appearance gives rise to a theory that they are of Semitic origin. Undoubtedly, in earlier times much of the Transvaal gold and copper trade passed through their hands, and the present Lemba may be the remnants of a large community of traders and metalworkers who were in close alliance with East Coast merchants and tolerated by the peoples of the interior on account of their industrial skills.

The successors of the Gokomere pottery makers were probably some ancestral Sotho peoples, whose descendants occupy much of the Transvaal, Orange Free State and Basutoland today. Nguni peoples were settled on the Natal coast by the end of the sixteenth century, but their origins are unknown. The Limpopo valley came under Karanga influence by the fourteenth century, whilst Europeans visited the Cape of Good Hope from the end of the fifteenth century onwards, and the Dutch settled there in 1652. The colonists gradually explored the interior and parties of Boer families made contact with Xhosa peoples near the Great Fish river in the early eighteenth century. Soon there was conflict between them over grazing lands, which led to almost continuous warfare between the two factions as European settlement expanded. The story of the nineteenth century in South Africa is one of continuous clashes between the interests of Boer and British and those of the Iron Age peoples who had been settled in the eastern, central and northern parts of the South African interior for many centuries.

CHAPTER XIII

The Nineteenth Century

THE EVENTS OF the closing century of the Iron Age were determined almost entirely by the efforts of one man, Shaka, born in a Zulu village in 1787. This child became the ruler of a vast Zulu empire, which extended from southern Mozambique in the north, southwards to the Bashee river and far into the Orange Free State and the Transvaal. At an early age, Shaka distinguished himself as a warrior in Chief Dingiswayo's regiments and developed the stabbing spear which revolutionized Zulu warfare, for it was an invincible weapon in the hands of Shaka's ruthlessly efficient *impis*. Shaka became the master of his neighbours and the logical successor of Dingiswayo, who was killed in 1818. By a series of ruthless campaigns, he extended Zulu influence over an enormous area. His empire survived until his assassination by Dingaan in 1828. He was succeeded by Dingaan who, however, had not the intelligence of his predecessor. Dingaan reigned for twelve years and his domains were gradually whittled away by European settlers. In the end he was defeated at the battle of Blood River by a combined force of Boers and Zulu *impis* under the command of Mpande, who succeeded him and reigned until 1872. Cetshwayo was the last of the independent Zulu kings, and came into conflict with the British in the Zulu war of 1879. As a result of this struggle the Zulu kingdom was finally broken.

Fig. 50

Shaka's empire-building efforts had widespread repercussions. One of the few peoples he or his generals did not succeed in conquering were the Basuto, who were effectively welded into a strong nation by the famous Chief Mosheshe. Mosheshe's policy was to create cultural and linguistic unity throughout his country. European missionaries were welcomed by Mosheshe in 1833, and Basutoland came under British rule during the late nineteenth century.

A number of Zulu leaders fled before the might of Shaka, taking with them detachments of their soldiers. A young Mumalo chieftain named Mzilikazi was entrusted with a small punitive campaign in the Transvaal in 1822. Upon its successful conclusion, he defied Shaka but was forced to flee northwards with his faithful warriors. In the following years he played havoc with the Sotho tribes of the Transvaal and his people became rich, acquiring the name Matabele, 'those who disappear out of sight behind their immense Zulu war-shields of stout cow hide'. By 1825, Mzilikazi was settled in the Central Transvaal, his regiments raiding Rhodesian kraals. Harassed by Dingaan's *impis* and Boer settlers, he wandered through eastern Bechuanaland and eventually settled near the Matopo Hills in Rhodesia about 1840, having left his mark on a vast tract of central Africa. The Rozwi *Mambos* of eastern Rhodesia were destroyed by Mzilikazi's *impis* and Ndebele (Matabele) rule was established over what is now known, appropriately, as Matabeleland. After the veteran chief's death in 1868, Lobengula was proclaimed king of the Ndebele domains. He extended the empire, his *impis* raiding far to the north and west of Bulawayo as well as north of the Zambezi.

Plate 52

Another chieftain who changed the lives of many people was Zwangendaba, who was driven northwards from Zulu country in 1821–2 as a result of an unsuccessful campaign against Shaka. He and his followers moved north along the Lubombo foothills to the lower Limpopo, devastating the regions through which they passed. Clashing with another Zulu leader named Nxaba, he pressed on northwards in 1826 or 1827. Zwangendaba and his Ngoni based themselves on the headwaters of the Sabi and laid waste the peaceful Karanga kingdom, destroying Zimbabwe in the early 1830's. In 1831, they ravaged the Rozwi centres of Matabeleland and, after

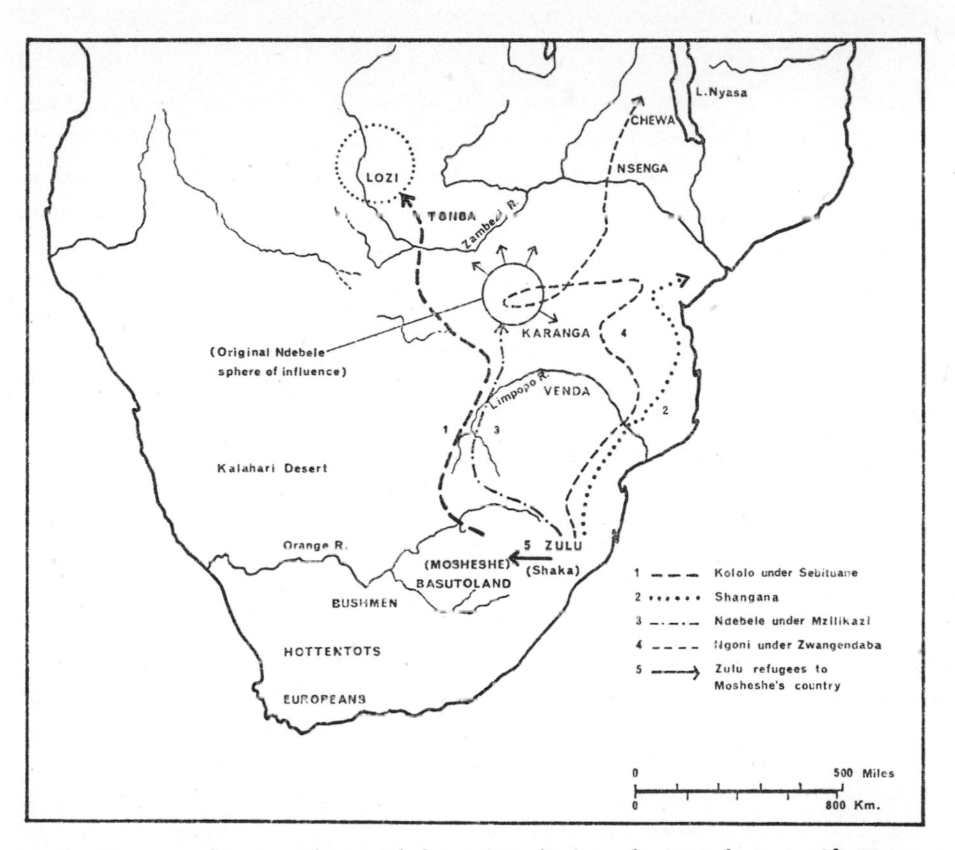

Fig. 50. Movements of Bantu peoples into Rhodesia and Zambia during the nineteenth century. After Fage, 1958

visiting the Limpopo valley, moved north and crossed the Zambezi near Zumbu on 28th November, 1835, during an eclipse of the sun. The Ngoni then descended on the tribes east of the Luangwa. After Zwangendaba's death in 1845, the horde split up, some moving to the Victoria Nyanza, others settling in Southern Malawi. Mpezeni, the principal chief and son of Zwangendaba, stayed in Zambia, raiding into Bemba and Bisa country and terrorizing a large area.

At the same time as the Ngoni were ravaging eastern Zambia, the Bemba were gaining in power. It will be recalled that the Portuguese at Tete had mounted a number of expeditions to Lunda country in an attempt to open up a route across to Angola. Their attempts had failed, but where the Portuguese faltered, the Arabs succeeded. By dint of astute political manoeuvring and by assimilating themselves with the local people, they were able to further their own ends. The Arabs, from Kilwa and Zanzibar, were interested in ivory, copper and the slaves to carry them. With the aid of the Yeke people of Katanga, they penetrated the domains of the Kazembe and the Bemba, trading firearms for ivory and slaves. The Bemba were not slow to take advantage of the superior qualities of these new weapons. In concert with their Arab allies, they ravaged most of the northern parts of Zambia between Lunda country and the Luangwa, providing slaves for the East Coast markets. It was upon this terrible trade that their prosperity depended, for their country was comparatively infertile, whereas the Lunda, whose influence gradually waned, had a favourable environment and no incentives to territorial expansion. Inevitably, there were clashes between the Ngoni and Bemba, which finally ended with the establishment of British rule in the 1890's.

Plate 51

At the beginning of the nineteenth century, the Lozi empire on the Upper Zambezi flood-plain was gradually expanded by means of an alliance between the ruling families and the Mbunda, who were skilled warriors, but this kingdom was overthrown by yet another remarkable leader.

Plate 54

Sebituane was a chief of the Bafokeng tribe, a group of Sotho peoples living near the Vet river in South Africa. Harried by devastating tribal raids in 1822, he led his people northwards into Bechuanaland, fighting with various tribes on the way, including Mzilikazi's *impis*. His people acquired the name Makololo during their wanderings. He pressed on in the direction of Damaraland and the Lake Ngami region, eventually reaching the banks of the Zambezi upstream of Kazungula in the early 1830's. Taking advantage of a tribal feud, he crossed the river with his people, defeated a large force of Tonga tribesmen and ranged northwards over the Batoka plateau towards Kafue. Worsted there by the Ndebele, he moved westwards, overthrowing the Lozi leaders in the 'Battle of Kataba', and, after a series of further campaigns, gained control of the Lozi kingdom. Sebituane governed his vast new domains by placing selected henchmen in the principal villages, as headmen. During the next decade he fought a series of battles with Mzilikazi's Ndebele, but managed to establish the Zambezi as his line of defence.

In 1851, Sebituane was visited by the missionary and explorer David Livingstone at his headquarters at Linyanti. The missionary and the chief became close friends, a friendship which was cut short by the latter's death in the same year. About the same time, Portuguese half-breed slave traders, named Mambari, visited Kololo country for the first time and attempted to trade firearms for slaves. They did not achieve the success of their Arab counterparts in Bemba country, and the trade was never on a large scale. Livingstone returned to Linyanti in 1853, and stayed for five months with the Kololo before setting out on his famous journey across Africa to Loanda and Quilimane in November 1853. The explorer reached the East Coast in May 1856, having explored most of the length of the Zambezi as well as the Batoka plateau. When Livingstone returned to Sesheke on his Zambezi expedition in 1860, he found Sekeletu, Sebituane's son, suffering from leprosy and the Kololo kingdom in dire straits. In 1863, Sekeletu died and the Kololo kingdom was overthrown in the following year by the Lozi leader Sipopa and his generals. Twenty-two years later, the Reverend F. Coillard founded his mission station at Sesheke.

Plate 56

Plate 55

The South African and Rhodesian interior was widely explored by settlers, missionaries and big-game hunters during the nineteenth century. Most of South Africa had been opened for European settlement by the 1890's and Cecil Rhodes negotiated a mineral agreement with the Ndebele chief Lobengula in 1890. The European settlement of Rhodesia followed soon afterwards. International interest in the potentiality of Zambia followed David Livingstone's explorations and, after various missionary endeavours and treaty-making expeditions, British rule was established north of the Zambezi in 1898. The Iron Age ended finally at the beginning of the present century, and Southern Africa entered a new period of economic and political development.

Plate 53

In the seventy-odd years since European government first reached all parts of Southern Africa, the face of the subcontinent has changed beyond all recognition. Traditional tribal structures and age-old population distributions have been destroyed or modified; industrial technology, urban settlement and education have revolutionized the lives of every inhabitant of Southern Africa. Man is no longer so dependent on the resources of his environment or on the labours of his hands to provide for all his needs. The events of the Iron Age have, however, played an important part in the development of modern political barriers and markets, and the recent history of the southern parts of Africa must, for all the protestations of politicians, be viewed against a background of the events of the last two thousand years.

Bibliography

Abreviations

J.A.H.	*Journal of African History*
Occ. P. Nat. Mus. S. Rhodesia	*Occasional Papers of the National Museum of Southern Rhodesia*
S.A.A.B.	*South African Archaeological Bulletin*

CHAPTER I

BENT, T. *The Ruined Cities of Mashonaland.* London, 1892.
CATON-THOMPSON, G. *The Zimbabwe Culture.* London, 1931.
FAGE, J. D. and OLIVER, R. *A Short History of Africa.* London, 1963.
HALL, R. N. *Great Zimbabwe.* London, 1905, and other works.
MCCALL, D. F. *Africa in Time Perspective.* Boston, 1964.
MACIVER, D. R. *Mediaeval Rhodesia.* London, 1906.
SUMMERS, R. *Zimbabwe, a Rhodesian Mystery.* Johannesburg, 1963.

CHAPTER II

BROOKS, C. E. P. *Climate through the Ages.* London, 1949.
CLARK, J. D. *The Prehistory of Southern Africa.* London, 1958.
COLE, M. *South Africa.* London, 1961.
SCHAPERA, I. *The Khoisan peoples of South Africa.* London, 1930.
WELLINGTON, J. H. *Southern Africa.* Cambridge, 1955.

CHAPTER III

CLARK, J. D. *The Stone Age Cultures of Northern Rhodesia.* Cape Town, 1950.
— *The Prehistory of Southern Africa.* London, 1958.
COOKE, C. K. Report on excavations at Pomongwe and Tsangula caves, Matopo Hills, Southern Rhodesia. *S.A.A.B.* XVIII (1963), 71, 75–171.

GABEL, C. Lochinvar Mound, a Later Stone Age camp-site in the Kafue Basin. *S.A.A.B.* XVIII (1963), 70, 40–8.

GOODWIN, A. J. H. and VAN RIET LOWE, C. *The Stone Age Cultures of South Africa.* Cape Town, 1929.

WILLCOX, A. *The Rock Art of South Africa.* Johannesburg, 1963.

CHAPTER IV

ARKELL, A. J. *Early Khartoum.* Oxford, 1949.

CLARK, J. D. *The Prehistory of Southern Africa.* London, 1958.

— The spread of food production into Sub-Saharan Africa. *J.A.H.* III, 2 (1962), 211–28.

— From Food Collecting to Incipient Urbanization in Africa South of the Sahara. In R. J. Braidwood, *Courses towards Urban Life.* Viking Fund Publications in Anthropology No. 32. New York, 1962.

— The Prehistoric origins of African culture. *J.A.H.* V, 2 (1964), 161–184.

— *The Kalambo Falls Prehistoric Site.* In preparation.

CLARK J. D. and FAGAN, B. M. Charcoals, Sands, and Channel-decorated pottery from Northern Rhodesia. *American Anthropologist.* In the press (1965).

GUTHRIE, M. Some developments in the prehistory of the Bantu language. *J.A.H.* III, 2 (1962), 273–82.

ROBINSON, K. R. An early Iron Age site from the Chibi District, Southern Rhodesia. *S.A.A.B.* XVI (1961), 75–102, 196.

— Further excavations in the Iron Age deposits at the Tunnel Site, Gokomere Hill, Southern Rhodesia. *S.A.A.B.* XVIII (1963), 160.

ROBINSON, K. R., SUMMERS, R. and WHITTY, A. *Zimbabwe Excavations, 1958.* Bulawayo, 1961.

SUMMERS, R. *Inyanga.* Cambridge, 1958.

CHAPTER V

DANIELS, S. G. H. The statistical determination of pottery types at the newly discovered Iron Age site of Dambwa, near Livingstone. *Proc. of the Central African Scientific and Medical Congress, Lusaka, 1963.* In the press, Oxford, 1965.

FAGAN, B. M. Pre-European ironworking in Central Africa. *J.A.H.* II, 2 (1961), 199–210.
— The Iron Age Sequence in the Southern Province of Northern Rhodesia. *J.A.H.* IV, 2 (1963), 157–77.
— *Iron Age Cultures in Zambia*, I. In the press (1965).
INSKEEP, R. R. Some Iron Age sites in Northern Rhodesia. *S.A.A.B.* XVII (1960), 67, 136–80.
WHITE, C. M. N. The Balovale Peoples and their historical background. *Human Problems in Central Africa*, VIII (1949), 26–41.

CHAPTER VI

FAGAN, B. M. The Greefswald sequence: Mapungubwe and Bambandyanalo. *J.A.H.* V, 3 (1964), 337–62.
FOUCHÉ, L. (ed.). *Mapungubwe*. Cambridge, 1937.
GARDNER, G. A. *Mapungubwe*, Vol. II. Pretoria, 1963.
GOODALL, E. Report on an Ancient Burial Ground, Salisbury, Southern Rhodesia. *Proc. 4th Pan-African Congress on Pre-history. Leopoldville, 1959*, II (1962), 315–22.
MENNELL, F. P. and SUMMERS, R. The 'Ancient Workings' of Southern Rhodesia. *Occ. P. Nat. Mus. S. Rhodesia*, 2, 20 (1955), 765–77.
ROBINSON, K. R. Four Rhodesian Iron Age Sites, an account of stratigraphy and finds. *Occ. P. Nat. Mus. S. Rhodesia*, 2, 22A (1958).
— *Khami Ruins*. Cambridge, 1959.
WHITTY, A. An Iron Age site at Coronation Park, Salisbury. *S.A.A.B.* XIII (1958), 10–20.

CHAPTER VII

AXELSON, E. *Portuguese in South East Africa, 1600–1700*. Johannesburg, 1960.
FAGAN, B. M. The Iron Age sequence in the Southern Province of Northern Rhodesia. *J.A.H.* IV, 2 (1963), 157–77.
— Northern Rhodesia 1,500 years ago. *Ill. London News*, 20th June, 1964.
— *Iron Age cultures in Zambia*, II. In preparation.

FREEMAN-GRENVILLE, G. S. P. *The Medieval history of the Tanganyika Coast.* Oxford, 1962.

MATHEW, A. G. and OLIVER, R. *History of East Africa,* Vol. I. Oxford, 1963.

ROBINSON, K. R. The Archaeology of the Rozwi. *Proc. of the Conference of the History of the Central African Peoples,* Lusaka, 1963.

CHAPTER VIII

CATON-THOMPSON, G. *The Zimbabwe Culture.* Oxford, 1931.

FOUCHÉ, L. *Mapungubwe.* Cambridge, 1937.

GARDNER, C. A. *Mapungubwe,* Vol. II. Pretoria, 1963.

ROBINSON, K. R., SUMMERS, R. and WHITTY, A. *Zimbabwe Excavations, 1958.* Bulawayo, 1961.

SCHOFIELD, J. F. *Primitive Pottery.* Cape Town, 1948.

WHITTY, A. A classification of Prehistoric Stone Buildings in Mashonaland, Southern Rhodesia. *S.A.A.B.* XIV (1959), 54, 57–71.

CHAPTER IX

In addition to the works under Chapter VII:

ABRAHAM, D. P. The early political history of the Kingdom of Mwene Mutapa, 850–1589. In *Historians in Tropical Africa,* Salisbury, 1960. 61–92.

— Maramuca, an exercise in the combined use of Portuguese Records and Oral Tradition. *J.A.H.* II, 2 (1961), 211–26.

AXELSON, E. *Portuguese in South East Africa, 1600–1700.* Johannesburg, 1960.

ROBINSON, K. R. *Khami Ruins.* Cambridge, 1959.

— The Archaeology of the Rozwi. *Proc. of the Conference of the History of the Central African Peoples.* Lusaka, 1963.

CHAPTER X

DOKE, C. M. *A comparative study of Shona phonetics.* Johannesburg, 1931.

KIRKMAN, J. S. *The Arab City of Gedi.* Oxford, 1954.

SUMMERS, R. *Inyanga.* Cambridge, 1958.

CHAPTER XI

BRELSFORD, W. V. *The tribes of Northern Rhodesia.* Lusaka, 1956.

CUNNISON, I. Kazembe and the Portuguese, 1798–1831. *J.A.H.* II, 1 (1961), 61 76.

FAGAN, B. M. The Iron Age of Northern Rhodesia. *Current Anthropology.* In the press (1964).

FAGE, J. D. and OLIVER, R. *A Short History of Africa.* London, 1963.

LANE POOLE, E. H. *The Native tribes of the Eastern Province of Northern Rhodesia.* Lusaka, 1938.

NENQUIN, J. *Excavations at Sanga, 1957.* Tervuren, 1963.

CHAPTER XII

BOXER, G. R. *The Tragic History of the Sea.* Hakluyt Society, London, 1959.

BRYANT, A. T. *Olden Times in Zululand and Natal.* London, 1929.

CAMPBELL, J. *Travels in South Africa,* London, 1822. Vol. 1.

HOEPEN, E. C. N. VAN and HOFFMAN, A. C. Die oorblyfsels van Buispoort en Braktaagte noord-wes wan Zeerust. *Archaeological Memoirs of the National Museum, Bloemfontein, South Africa.* 2, 1935.

MASON, R. J. *The Prehistory of the Transvaal.* Johannesburg, 1962.

SCHAPERA, I. (ed). *The Bantu-speaking tribes of Southern Africa.* London, 1937.

SCHOFIELD, J. F. *Primitive Pottery.* Cape Town, 1948.

SOGA, J. H. *The South-Eastern Bantu.* Johannesburg, 1930.

STAYT, H. A. *The BaVenda.* Oxford, 1931.

WILSON, M. The Early History of the Transkei and Ciskei. *African Studies,* 18, 4 (1959), 167–79.

CHAPTER XIII

BRELSFORD, W. V. *The tribes of Northern Rhodesia.* Lusaka, 1956.

BRYANT, A. T. *Olden Times in Zululand and Natal.* London, 1929.

ELLENBERGER, D. F. *History of the Basuto.* London, 1912.

LIVINGSTONE, D. *Missionary travels and researches in South Africa.* London, 1857.

LIVINGSTONE, C. and D. *Narrative of an expedition to the Zambezi and its tributaries.* London, 1865.

Radiocarbon dates

Lists of radiocarbon dates for the Iron Age in Sub-Saharan Africa are regularly published in the *Journal of African History*, and the reader is referred to that Journal for details.

Sources of Illustrations

I am grateful to the following for kindly supplying me with photographs: Mr David Attenborough, pl. 24, 25; Mr C. K. Cooke, pl. 2, 35–41; Mr C. S. Holliday, pl. 1, 4–6, 8, 9, 18, 20, 21, 32, 47, 48; Dr R. J. Mason, pl. 49, 50; National Archives, Salisbury, pl. 51, 52, 55; The Livingstone Museum, pl. 12–16, 19, 31, 53; Rhodesia National Tourist Board, pl. 23, 26–28, 33, 34, 42; Roan Selection Trust Ltd, pl. 7; South African Museum, Cape Town, pl. 29, 30; Mr Eric Woods, Express Services, Livingstone, pl. 10, 11, 46; Zambia Information Services, pl. 3, 43, 44, 54; and the National Monuments Commission, pl. 17, 22, 45.

Grateful acknowledgement is also due to the following authors and publishers for permission to reproduce text figures from their works: Edward Arnold Ltd, fig. 45; Associated Book Publishers Ltd, fig. 36, 49; Mr M. C. Burkitt, fig. 5, 6; Cambridge University Press, fig. 5, 6; Professor J. Desmond Clark, fig. 3, 4, 7; Professor Monica Cole, fig. 49; Director of Museums, Southern Rhodesia, fig. 24, 34, 35, 37; Professor J. D. Fage, fig. 45; Historical Monuments Commission, Southern Rhodesia, fig. 21, 32, 39, 42; The Trustees of the Inyanga Research Fund, fig. 15, 44; The Editors, *Journal of African History*, fig. 7; The Museum Trustees of Kenya, fig. 10; Dr L. S. B. Leakey, fig. 10; Miss H. R. MacCalman, fig. 8; The Editor of *Man*, fig. 12; Thomas Nelson and Sons (Africa) Ltd, fig. 47; Penguin Books Ltd, fig. 3, 30; Dr Merrick Posnanaky, fig. 9; University of Pretoria, fig. 25, 26; Mr K. R. Robinson, fig. 14, 21, 34, 35, 39, 42; Dr C. A. Schoute-Vanneck, fig. 48; The South African Archaeological Society, fig. 13, 14, 43, 48; Mr Roger Summers, fig. 15, 23, 24; The Editor, Uganda Journal, fig. 9; Mr A. Whitty, fig. 27, 31, 43; and Mr A. Willcox, fig. 47.

Fig. 12, 13, 22, 33, 38, 40, 41 are drawn from specimens in the collections of the Livingstone Museum.

Chatto and Windus Ltd kindly allowed me to quote the passage on p. 154 from *The Matabele Journals of Robert Moffat*, ed. J. P. R. Wallis.

THE PLATES

2
3

A man and woman att the Cape of good Hope
The Table
Herberts mount
Suger Loafe
K.C.
James mount
Souldanja bay

5

6

7
8
9

10
11

12

13

14

15
16

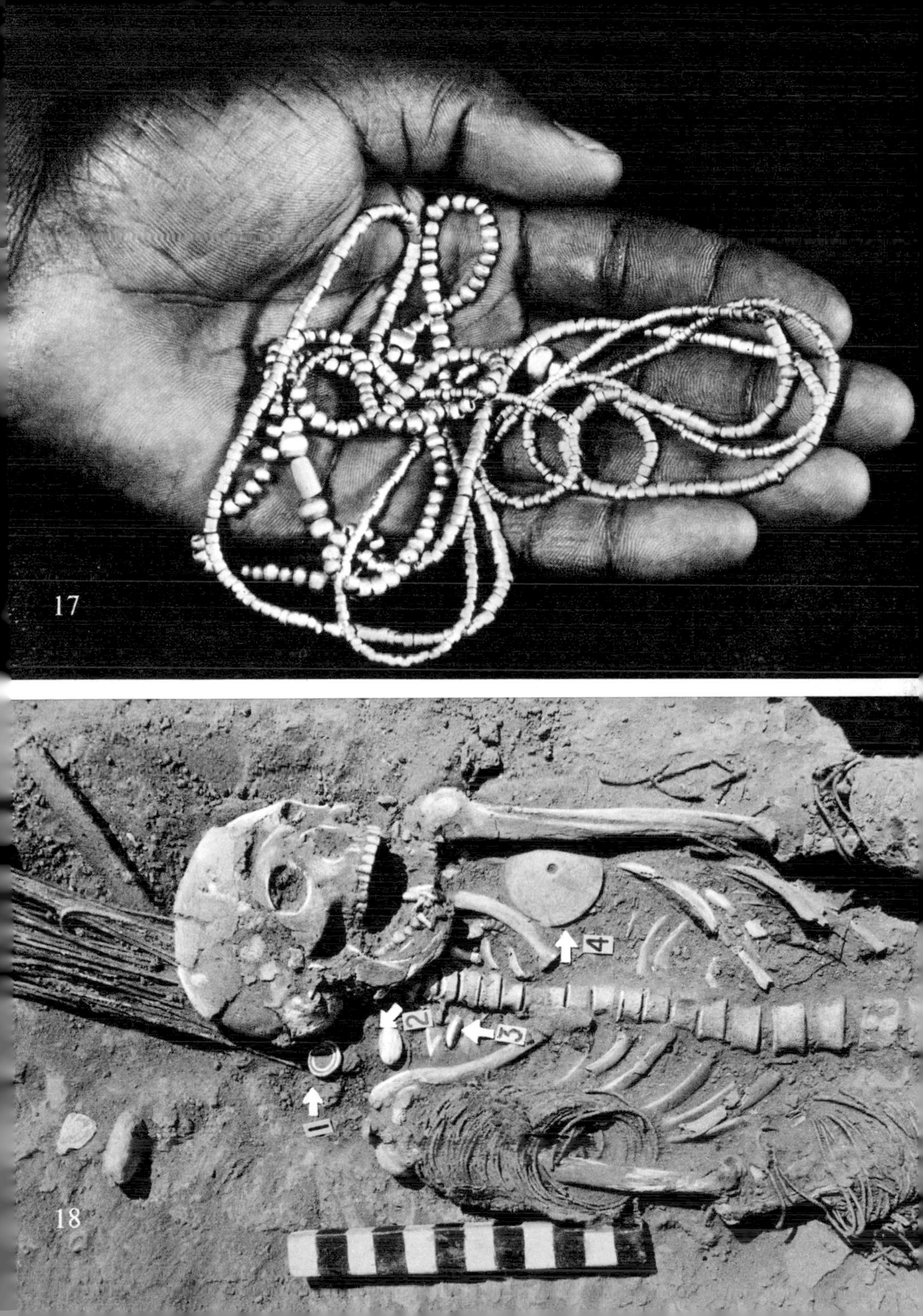
17
18
1
2
3
4

19

21
22

23

24
25

26
27

28
29
30

31
32
R. Coanza
to be the same Nation
elsewhere call'd Galles
It is not known where
the River Cuneni has its rise
R. Cuneni or the great River
Proyce of Genge
or Quillenge
Zemba
catir
COUNTRY OF JAGA CASANGE
KINGDOM
OF CHICOVA
where are many
Silver Mines
Cataracts
Chicova
Salt
Fountain
Coty OF Y MUMBOS
Antropophages
or Men-eaters
COTRY.
Km OF SACOMBA
Chicorongo
Call'd by the Cafres the Back bone of the World
Cafres Allys to the
Portuguese
Tete or
Santiago
Lake & M. of
Rufumbo
Fountn Macnbe
THE ZIMBAS
or MUZIMBAS
Antropophages or Men eaters
they pay divine worship to
their King.
Fortress of the
Zimbas
KINGDOM
OF
MONGALE
haveing a great
number of Subjects
R. Mongale
Maçuas
C. del gado
Malinda
Macoloe
Matemo I.
Illands of
Quirinba
Chaga Bay
Fungo Bay
Residence
of Mauruca
Km OF MAURUCA
which commands
part of the Macuas
K. Angoche
M. of Chiri
very fertile
and Populouse
Cafres Allys to
the Portuguese
Sena
M. Furs
Gold mine
Km OF MONGAS
Mount of Lupata
Km INHAMIOR
destroy'd by the
Monomotapa
Bocuto or
Manzovo
Gold M.
KINGDOM
OF ABUTUA
call'd by some
TOROA
It is rich in Gold
Mines
It is not yet discov-
er'd where ye River
Couama has
its Rise.
ESTATES OF MONOMOTAPA
Chetuchin
Royal City of
Monomotapa
Fatuca
Independent Cafres
Forest of Zebe
Km OF QUITEVE
Quitiqui
Gold mines
Zimbaoe
Residence of
Quiteve
R. Sofala
SOFALA
Bovor
Kilimane
Guloa Km
of the
Macuas
Luabo I.
Luabo R.
Inhaquea
Banck of Sofala
GULF OF SOFALA
MOZAMBIC
Shelss of Judia
Km OF MANICA
the King of which
calls himself
CHICANGA
Manica or
Magnica
Gold mines
of Manica
Coty of Quloane
Km OF SABIA
OR SEDANDA
Coty of Sogna
Botonga
Tonge
Km OF INHAMBANE
R. and Pt
of Inhambana
C. Courans
Inhampura R.
Ouro R.
Maonica or R. of St Espirit
Inhaqua I.
Inhaqua here beguins the
Gouvernment of Mozambic
R. of Laurence Marquez
COUNTRY OF
KING BIRI
THE
CABONAS
Antropophages
or Men-eaters
THE
CHAINOUQUAS
Rich in Cattle
a Lagod
or the Lake
Coty of Zanguane
Ladraon R.
THE HEUSAQUAS
This Nation make use
of Lyons in fighting
HOTTENTOTS
Terra dos
Naonetas
St Lucia B.
Pequeno R.
Porto Pequeria
CAFRERIA
MAGUAS
P. S. Augus
Py of Nasumento
I.S. Jaque
P. S. Jaque

33

34

35

36

37
38

39

40

41
42

43

44

45

46
47
48

49
50

51

52
53

54
55

Notes on the Plates

Many of the plates are intended to show aspects of day-to-day life during the Iron Age. In some of the pictures, modern clothing and utensils can be seen. No attempt has been made to recall modes of dress and customs which have now been forgotten. The plates serve to show the continuity of the Iron Age with the twentieth century.

1 Kalambo Falls near Abercorn in Zambia. The Stone and Iron Age sites are in the ancient lake basin immediately behind the falls, p. 54.

2 Tropical woodland with a herd of elephant. Southern Africa is rich in game and vegetable resources, p. 24.

3 Later Stone Age rock paintings from Silozwane Cave, Matopo Hills, Rhodesia, p. 41.

4 Two Hottentots, depicted in Thomas Herberts' *Some Years' Travels into Africa and Asia* (1638), p. 30.

5 A Lozi man, showing characteristic Negro features, p. 30.

6 A Bushman woman, p. 30.

7 A Kaonde copper miner, p. 30.

8 Hoeing, the basic activity of Iron Age farmers. Cultivation is normally carried out by the women, p. 32.

9 Pounding *mugongo* nuts. Vegetable foods from the bush were an important part of Iron Age diet, p. 32.

10 Hut building in the traditional manner. The circle of poles has been erected and the piles of hut mud lie by the side, p. 32.

11 Women fishing with baskets in Barotseland, p. 32.

24 Zimbabwe Ruins. The Acropolis from the air, showing the Western Enclosure, p. 104.

25 Zimbabwe Ruins. The Temple from the air with the Conical Tower in the foreground. The sloping gradient of the enclosure wall can be clearly seen, p. 112.

26 Zimbabwe Ruins. The Conical Tower and traces of houses, p. 112.

27 Zimbabwe Ruins. The Wall of the Great Enclosure, with chevron pattern, p. 112.

28 Decorated soapstone dish from Zimbabwe. South African Museum, Cape Town. Height: *c.* 4 in., p. 114.

29 A soapstone bird from Zimbabwe. South African Museum, Cape Town. Height of bird: *c.* 12 in., p. 114.

30 Zimbabwe Ruins. The Western Enclosure on the Acropolis, from which the crucial stratigraphical evidence was obtained, p. 106.

31 Mapungubwe Hill from the south-west. The burial area is towards the western end of the hill, p. 116.

32 Map of Southern Africa by John Senex (fl. 1690–1740), dated to 1720. This shows the kingdom of Monomotapa, Zimbabwe (Zimboe), Manica, Sena and Tete, Butua and the Zimbas (Anthropophages or Men-eaters). John Senex was a well-known cartographer in the early eighteenth century, p. 128.

33 Nalatale Ruins, Rhodesia, occupied by the Rozwi in the seventeenth and eighteenth centuries, p. 124.

34 Decorated walling at Nalatale, p. 124.

35 Dhlo-Dhlo Ruins, Rhodesia, p. 124.

52 Ndebele warriors dancing a war dance, p. 168.

53 A hippopotamus hunt. This nineteenth-century print vividly depicts the dangers of the pastime, much practised amongst Zambezi tribes, p. 172.

54 The Lozi Royal Barge in which the Paramount Chief moves from his summer to his winter palace, across the flooded Barotse plain. Forty paddlers propel the barge, p. 170.

55 A trench at the Behrens site, a nineteenth-century Tonga village on the Batoka plateau, Zambia. This shows the shallow deposits typical of more recent Iron Age sites. In the foreground, traces of a hearth and a grain bin. A large midden in the background, p. 171.

56 David Livingstone, by J. A. Whymper. From a photograph taken by T. Annan, p. 171.

Index